1974

To John Anthony

Build men,
who love Him,
His... yours,

Wayland Moore

2 Tim 2:1-4

PSA-116

New Testament Follow-Up
For Pastors and Laymen

New Testament Follow-Up

For Pastors and Laymen

*How to Conserve, Mature, and
Multiply the Converts*

by

WAYLON B. MOORE

WM. B. EERDMANS COMPANY
GRAND RAPIDS, MICHIGAN

ISBN 0-8028-1136-1

First printing, July 1963
Second printing, October 1964
Third printing, May 1968
Fourth printing, August 1969
Revised edition, July 1970
Sixth printing, November 1972
Seventh printing, March 1973

PHOTOLITHOPRINTED BY CUSHING - MALLOY, INC.
ANN ARBOR, MICHIGAN, UNITED STATES OF AMERICA

Dedicated to

Bruce, Dennis, Harry, Daws, Bill, Charlie, and Bob, men of God who shared with me their life in Christ; and to the pastors and missionaries whose response to follow-up will produce disciples for Him.

Introduction

The greatest problem the majority of our churches face today is that of conserving and enlisting the people we win to Christ and the church. Frankly, everywhere I go this is the number-one "headache."

Pastors and other church leaders are literally overwhelmed with the problem of enlistment. Many of us feel like throwing up our hands and crying, "What's the use?" This feeling of frustration is due to two facts. First, we do not know how to conserve the results of our evangelistic fervor. Second, we are not willing to pay the price of a dedicated and thorough follow-up with our new members. Therefore we are losing too many of them.

Rev. Waylon Moore has given us a splendid book on this subject. It is both practical and idealistic. It is full of unique ideas, and Rev. Moore is careful to stress that his plans will not work unless they are worked.

Get this book. It will disturb and challenge you to do something about the huge "back door" problem.

— RAMSEY POLLARD, PASTOR
Bellevue Baptist Church
Memphis, Tennessee

Foreword

Today there is an increasing emphasis on evangelism. Denominational leaders around the world are in agreement that the church must evangelize or die. To make sure that this emphasis is carried out, many seminaries today have a Chair of Evangelism. Most denominations have men appointed full time to this field. Evangelistic missions are commonplace and visitation evangelism is fast becoming a part of every regular church program.

Much effort is being made, then, to reach people with the message of salvation, and, from all reports, with wonderful success. What happens to these who are coming to Christ as new-born babes is of utmost importance. Whether they go on to grow spiritually and become effective Christians will be determined by the amount of care that is given them after their decision. Someone has said that the end result of evangelism is an informed Christian who, in turn, has become a witness. Another has said that the decision is 5 percent, but the living out of that decision is 95 percent. When a child is born into the human family, the work has just begun for his parents. This child needs feeding, protecting, and training. A person born into the family of God needs the same tender care over a long period until he becomes established in the church and is able intelligently to vocalize his faith. "Be ready always to give an answer to every man that asketh you a reason of the hope that is in you with meekness and fear" (I Pet. 3:15).

Here is a book that should be most helpful in following up "young believers." I have known the writer for a number of years and find him to be a man of God with a keen vision for follow-up. Over the years he has had much experience in this work and has compiled very helpful material in this field. You will find that Mr. Moore focuses his attention on the individual — how to reach him with the gospel message, how to train him for Christian service, and then how to put him to work in evangelism. Certainly the emphasis should be on the individual, for we find that people differ and at times need individual care to meet their need.

Here, then, is a book that I would highly recommend to pastors and teachers alike. I believe that if the suggestions and instructions are carefully followed, it can only result in blessing for the church.

Charles Riggs, Director
Counseling and Follow-up,
Billy Graham Team

Preface

As a Christian, you have been assigned by your Lord to the biggest job in the world: winning souls to Jesus Christ and helping to develop them into the image of their Saviour. Through you and your church hundreds of men and women can become ablaze for the Lord, their lives transformed by the application of New Testament principles. I have seen it happen. These "follow-up" principles and some methods of applying them form the content of this book. It is no mere listing of what we need to do but a manual of step-by-step instruction on how to do it.

Although the word "follow-up" does not appear in the Bible, we have firm Biblical grounds for using it, because it is a basic idea which is to be found throughout the New Testament. It is the process of training and bringing spiritual children to a place of mature fellowship with Christ and service in the church. It embraces all we do individually or collectively to integrate the new converts into the church, to keep them enlisted, to build them up spiritually, and to teach them to win others to Christ.

The great task of our churches is not only the salvation of souls but also the maturation of believers unto Christlike living. This dual task is exemplified in the New Testament, and it can be accomplished only through applying New Testament follow-up principles. Some churches are already applying these principles; other churches have not yet seen their scope and value. The suggestions and ideas presented in this book come from God's Word and have been tested and proved effective today in large city churches as well as in small country churches, and also on the mission fields of the world.

If these New Testament principles are applied consistently, they will (1) deepen your personal relationship with the Lord and your understanding of His divine plan for reaching the world, (2) integrate the new Christians into the total program of the church, (3) stimulate them to go on with Christ and grow spiritually, (4) increase the church membership by encouraging them to witness and by re-enlisting other Christians in soul-winning and building up the body of Christ. These benefits are all interrelated, and may be accomplished simultaneously.

The ideas in this book are presented in a practical form so that they can be applied when working with an individual, a class, or the whole church. Underlying everything suggested here are three imperatives for an effective program of follow-up in the local church:

1. Every believer must be helped to feed daily on the Word of God and apply it constantly to his daily life.
2. The pastor must re-emphasize in his own ministry the need of spending time with individuals, "discipling men."
3. The membership must learn that spiritually qualified people rather than organizations win and develop individual disciples.

Do not hurry from chapter to chapter. At the end of some chapters related Bible-study questions are given to re-emphasize the scriptural truths in the chapter. Because of the wide scope of the material, many chapters are simply introductory since space prohibits exhaustive treatment of the various topics. But consult the Word, as did those at Berea who "searched the scriptures daily, whether those things were so" (Acts 17:11). If this book does no more than cause you to seek the Lord and His Word for these basic principles, then the author will feel richly rewarded for his efforts. Prayerfully consider your own needs, the needs of your church, and the tragic plight of the millions who have yet to hear the gospel.

I owe very much to the personal ministry of Dawson Trotman and the Navigators. It was Daws whose life and message first caused me to focus attention on follow-up, and it was he who urged me to use New Testament follow-up principles in my church.

My thanks go also to Dr. C. E. Autrey who in 1958 encouraged me to put my experiences in this field in book form.

Writing this book would not have been possible without the constant encouragement of my wife, Clemmie E. Moore, M.D., who spent months helping me to organize this material on "spiritual pediatrics." And, finally, it was Miss Arline Harris whose editorial suggestions brought the book to completion.

—Waylon B. Moore

Contents

PART I

CHAPTER 1

Conserve, Mature, and Multiply

Follow-up is the conservation, maturation, and multiplication of the fruit of evangelism. Winning and building are inseparably linked together in the Scriptures. There is no continuing New Testament evangelism without follow-up. They are God's "two-edged sword" for reaching men and making them effective disciples for Christ.

A certain missionary group has as its goal "systematic evangelism and synchronized follow-up." The two go together like the two rails of a train track; a break in either stops forward progress. Like the sowing, watering, and reaping of evangelism, follow-up takes time; it is not an act, but a process. There is no quick way to spiritual maturity and Christlikeness.

The New Testament Example

No other subject is more widely taught and illustrated in the New Testament than personal, consistent, church-integrated follow-up. Most of the epistles of Paul, Peter, and John are follow-up letters to those new in the faith. Paul exclaimed, "So, naturally, we proclaim Christ! We warn everyone we meet, and we teach everyone we can, all that we know about him" (Col. 1:28, Phillips). Through "warning" the evangelistic message is proclaimed; through "teaching" those won are brought into the fullness of life in Christ.

The spread of the gospel in the first century was amazing. Those early disciples obeyed their Lord's command to go into all the world, preaching and teaching, until their contemporaries complained that "they . . . have turned the world upside down" (Acts 17:6). How did this small group (only 120 at Pentecost) grow to such proportions of power and boldness? These early soul-winners were also church-planters; they were not satisfied with merely making converts. They exalted a living Saviour and implanted into their converts truths from God which made them life-changers and nation-changers. To them, being a Christian meant having a vital relationship with a risen Christ. His power flowing through them was irresistible. But what of us today?

Though this power is still available it is not being used effectively by the average Christian. God cannot be glorified in men and women who have been believers for years and yet are living and thinking and reacting to the situations of life just the same way they did when they first trusted in Christ. Through follow-up, a consistent program of maturing new converts can be carried on as a vital part of the total church ministry. Adequate follow-up is the most effective method of bringing indifferent members back to Christ-centered living.

There is too frequently a lack of follow-up even in strong missionary churches. For one thing, pastors are not agreed on what constitutes an adequate church follow-up. In comparison with New Testament standards, let us look at some of the things that follow-up is not. It is not giving a new Christian a pep talk on Bible reading or emphasizing the imperative of stewardship, important as these things may be. Neither is it loading him down with tracts and pamphlets. Follow-up is more than getting the new believer to hear the Sunday sermon or join a Sunday-school class; it is more than repeated attempts to enlist him in the activities of the church. These efforts are of value, but they neither meet the deepest needs of the new believer nor measure up to the scriptural standard.

All follow-up is directed in the New Testament toward the needs of the individual. Through the preaching, teaching, and training services of the church, principles of follow-up may be applied to the group, but always in the context of the individual life of each member of the group. In this day of mass dynamics and group thinking throughout our social structure, it must be constantly emphasized that our neglected spiritual resource for world evangelism is the layman who has been given adequate scriptural follow-up care. He is the shortest and most effective avenue to evangelizing the area of a church's influence. The personal aspect of follow-up is our point of greatest weakness and should become our major concern.

Conserving and Maturing Members

Many churches are growing increasingly concerned, and with good reason, about the discrepancy between the number on their church roll and their average attendance. It has been said that 40 percent of those joining the church each year are being lost to the program and influence of the church within ten years.[1] Dr. Roland Q. Leavell lists in round percentages the status of the church:

20 percent never pray
25 percent never read their Bible
30 percent never attend church
40 percent never give to any cause
50 percent never go to Sunday school
60 percent never attend evening services
70 percent never give to missions
80 percent never go to prayer meeting
90 percent never have family worship
95 percent never win a soul to Christ[2]

And, we might add, 99 percent never spend time following up the souls they have won to the Lord. Of the faithful who are enlisted in the program of the church, few have proved to be consistent soul-winners and disciple-builders.

Recently I heard a pastor decry the fact that out of a thousand in his Sunday school, he knew of only two laymen who were winning souls. "Short cuts in conservation are costing Southern Baptists alone, today, over 200,000 converts and

[1] Leonard Sanderson, *Personal Evangelism*, p. 114.
[2] Roland Q. Leavell, *The Romance of Evangelism*, p. 89.

$156,000,000 annually,"[3] writes Dr. C. E. Autrey, Secretary of Evangelism for Southern Baptists.

It is self-evident that large majorities of our church members are spiritually immature. As Paul puts it, "Are ye not carnal and walk as men?" (I Cor. 3:3). They are ignorant of the basic doctrines of the Bible, and what doctrine they do know they are unable to apply to their own experience. They equate Christianity with Sunday church attendance; in other words, they are spiritual babies that need to grow up.

But babies do not grow automatically; they must have food and care and training. When children are born into the physical world, God's plan is that each should have two parents. Most newborn children of God do not have even one spiritual foster father or mother who will give them parental care. It is unnatural and unhealthy for a new Christian to have to spend years in church without any consistent individual training outside a group situation. Neglected children usually become delinquent, and neglect of spiritual parental care is one reason why we have thousands of delinquent members on our church rolls.

A child needs to be led into a life of maturity over a period of time by careful and loving discipline if he is to become a good citizen. In the same way, a person's fruitfulness for Christ is almost always in proportion to the consistency and maturity of the spiritual parental care he has received. It is God's will that all believers should become mature. Follow-up will develop spiritual maturity in the church membership.

Multiplying the Ministry

God always intended that His work should be carried on by the individual Christians, and not be left entirely to the pastor. Most of the commands in the New Testament were given to all Christians, not just to the church leaders. The longer we cling to a sharp laity-clergy division, neglecting to develop lay leadership through personal training and follow-up, the

---

3 C. E. Autrey, *Basic Evangelism*, p. 148.

farther we lag behind in the great task of evangelizing the world.

The average pastor today is so busy with many different things that the fast pace at which he works not only jeopardizes his personal spiritual life but also puts him at a disadvantage in personally training an evangelistic-minded leadership in his church. He has to spend so much time just keeping the church alive and together that he has little time left to disciple those few individuals who might be able to assume some of his many responsibilities. Only by applying follow-up principles can the pastor realize the full potential of the membership for evangelism.

Today we speak of "exploding populations" and that means, to the Christian, that millions are being born, live, and die without ever having heard of Christ. Only through follow-up can the church multiply and strengthen its soul-winning to catch up with the staggering proportion of the unsaved. Soul-winning without follow-up has always failed in its objective of world evangelism. At best, it is the mere addition of souls to the church; few of them ever win others. Follow-up will change addition into multiplication in soul-winning.

Among those in the church who are spiritually healthy and mature, there are many who can be trained to care for the new and the immature Christians. Through application of New Testament principles of follow-up, the pastor will be able to conserve the membership that might otherwise become unenlisted, deepen the spiritual life of the active membership, strengthen his ministry with the laymen, and perpetuate his vision for reaching the community and the world for Christ.

Questions to Answer

1. What is God's purpose for every believer? (Eph. 4:13).
2. How did Paul interpret this goal? (Col. 1:28, 29).
3. How is this goal realized in the believer? (Jas. 1:22).
4. What is one difference between the spiritually mature and the immature? (Heb. 5:14; I Cor. 3:1-4, 18, 21,).

Questions for Meditation and Application

1. What percentage of your church membership would you estimate to be mature in Christ? Why so few?

2. Pause to think through the definition of follow-up at the opening of this chapter. As you start this book, which part of follow-up needs greater attention in your church?

CHAPTER 2

Caring for the Individual

Follow-up has been called "spiritual pediatrics." It is the parental care given new believers to bring them to spiritual maturity and fruitfulness. Billy Graham has said that all evangelism is personal; the mass approach merely channels the "seeker" to the soul-winner. Follow-up is also intensely personal. Instead of the group approach used in some churches, there is an increasing need for re-emphasizing the personal aspect of follow-up care. The Scriptures stress that Jesus was pre-eminently concerned with the individual. He expressed His parent-heart in acts and words of love and care for each individual disciple.

Unfortunately, few people demonstrate Christlike love for others and few understand the great and limitless field of ministry through the individual approach. Not many are willing to give that parental care which keeps the new convert from becoming a spiritual orphan. When the pastor and staff of a church must shoulder the full responsibility of caring for the new converts, the result is an orphanage situation. That is the situation in many churches, where converts are simply added to the body and are expected to look after themselves spiritually. Indeed, many are the orphans and few are the spiritual parents in the church.

Paul considered himself a parent to those he won to Christ. To the Corinthians he wrote, "For though ye have ten thousand instructors in Christ, yet have ye not many fathers, for in Christ Jesus I have begotten you through the gospel" (I Cor. 4:15). He also called those he won to Christ his own children at Galatia and Thessalonica (Gal. 4:19; I Thess. 2:11). Paul called Timothy and Titus his "sons" in the faith. As the Father has committed the "word of reconciliation" to Christians, so He has also entrusted to them the care of those new in the faith.

There are two ways to become a foster parent to spiritual babies: win them or adopt them. A spiritual parent assumes the care of those he leads to Christ, and the mature Christian with a parent-heart "adopts" a new believer or an immature fellow-believer who desires spiritual growth.

The Need for Love

Parents are responsible for loving, feeding, protecting and training their children until they reach maturity. Spiritually, every soulwinner has this fourfold responsibility. Jesus said, "This is my commandment, that ye love one another, as I have loved you" (John 15:12). Spiritual parents are to love their children as Christ loved them; this love is the basic necessity for successful parenthood, and is usually missing in follow-up that fails.

Feeding, protecting, and training, without love, will produce unbalanced, distorted lives in the spiritual realm as well as in the natural. Christlike love is to be the foundation of all attempts to give parental care to spiritual babies. Such love involves laying down one's life for another, if necessary. "Hereby perceive we the love of God, because he laid down his life for us: and we ought to lay down our lives for the brethren" (I John 3:16). A true parent never regrets the time, cost, or sacrifice necessary in bringing up spiritual children.

Since knowledge precedes love, time must be spent with the new convert to get to know him and to love him. Love grows as the life in Christ is shared from week to week. Love may be expressed in a sermon, but it can be demonstrated only in real life. This foundation of love prepares the new convert for balanced spiritual growth.

The Need for Nourishment

The babe in Christ also needs to be fed regularly with the right kind of food. In John 21 Jesus commanded Peter three times to feed His sheep and His lambs. We need to make sure, however, that we have the right spiritual formula for infant feeding; the only right food for the babe in Christ is the "milk of the word" (I Pet. 2:2). Nothing must take the place of the Bible in the daily spiritual diet of every believer. We feed ourselves physically about three times a day. A daily diet of the Word will help the new believer grow steadily and healthily. Pointing out the need for spiritual food, or telling the new Christian he must study the Bible, is not the same as teaching him how to get spiritual nourishment from the Scriptures.

A newborn baby receives milk from the bottle. Later on he is trained in right eating habits and choosing the right food and shown where to find it. In adolescence he not only eats food prepared by others, but also learns to cook some of his own food. A mature person is able to feed himself and others, and can teach others how to do the same. One who cannot feed himself is either a baby or an invalid.

Maturity in spiritual things enables a church member to be self-sustaining from the Word of God and to share his abundance with others. A mature Christian, living "by every word that proceedeth out of the mouth of God" (Matt. 4:4), is able to project the Christian doctrine and the program of the church into the whole world.

The Need for Protection

A new convert needs to be protected to ensure his spiritual growth. It is still true that Satan "as a roaring lion, walketh about, seeking whom he may devour" (I Pet. 5:8). This enemy of the soul considers no prey more tempting than the spiritual life of a new believer. The newborn child of God is in open season for all the ravages of Satan, and can easily be crippled spiritually for life.

The major areas of temptation in which Satan attempts to ensnare the believer are sex, security, and success: "the lust of the flesh, and the lust of the eyes, and the pride of life" (I John 2:16). These temptations can be withstood only by the shield of faith, which comes through the Word of God. Satan's first aim is to separate the convert from the Word, to starve him into weakness, and to keep him from availing himself of God's protection. One of the major duties of a spiritual parent is to teach his child how to meet temptations with the Word of God.

The spiritual parent also teaches protection by his own example. Through association the child absorbs the same spiritual habits which have brought victory to the parent. A child is also protected by instruction and warning given before he has to meet a situation of possible danger. He needs to be disciplined and to be rebuked for disobedience. "Whom the Lord loveth, he chasteneth." Discipline must be given in love, personally and privately, and must be centered on the commandments of God which have been broken.

Children who are uncared for, undisciplined, and unprotected become useless members of society. Lack of Christian care and discipline has ruined thousands of Christian lives, hindered the spread of the gospel and made stumbling blocks out of those who should be steppingstones. Parental protection by instruction, example, rebuke, and discipline prepares the convert for a useful, balanced, victorious Christian life.

The Need for Training

Parental care always involves training the baby, beginning when he is very young and intensifying it as he grows up. Spiritual parents also train their children, building on the foundation that is Christ Jesus. Paul warned in I Corinthians 3:10-15 that such building into lives is a grave responsibility. Some people use eternal materials to build with, and their work endures; others try to build with superficialities which can never stand the test of fire or equip for the pressures and adversities of this life. The quality of the building materials is of the utmost importance. The spiritual parent builds lives with eternal materials that can withstand trial and temptation.

The building materials comparable to "gold, silver, and

precious stones" are the basic doctrines of the Bible. The new believer needs to be taught not only the doctrines of assurance, prayer, and victory over sin, but also how to apply them in his daily life and how to teach them to others. Suggestions for training materials are found in the Appendices.

The test of successful training is the convert's stability under pressure. In I Thessalonians 3:5 Paul said that the effectiveness of his work among them was measured by their ability to live in victory over sin. If they did not have that victory in their lives, he felt that his work had been in vain. Another test of solid spiritual building is resultant witnessing. Paul emphasized that unless the Philippians were witnessing by life and by word to those in darkness, his work had been in vain (Phil. 2:15-16). Walking in victory and witnessing for Christ comprise the New Testament objectives of the training of new believers.

Bringing Children to Maturity

All that is done in the life of the believer to bring him to spiritual maturity and Christlikeness is New Testament follow-up. Paul's goal was that every one of his converts should be "mature in Christ Jesus" (Col. 1:28). In Ephesians 4:13 he emphasized that ideal: "Till we all come in the unity of the faith, and of the knowledge of the Son of God, unto a perfect man, unto the measure of the stature of the fulness of Christ." Most churches are grateful for the leadership of a few mature believers, but God's plan is that all should be mature.

Christian maturity is the knowledge of Bible doctrines consistently applied to life situations, not head-knowledge. Maximum maturity is attained by the continual control of the Holy Spirit in the Christian's life, molding him into the image of Christ.

Through careful follow-up, a child of God is guided into spiritual maturity. The goal of follow-up in the church is to have every believer walking in obedience to the Word and in victory. This work must be started by those who are mature, the pastor and the church leaders, and be expanded until at last every member is actively participating. Leaders must have parent-hearts, and put into effect a program of individual follow-up that provides love, food, protection, and training to the immature and to the new babes in Christ.

Questions to Answer

1. What is the proper food for the babe in Christ? (I Pet. 2:2; Heb. 5:13).

2. What are some marks of a mature believer? (II Cor. 5:7; Matt. 4:4; I Thess. 5:18; II Cor. 9:17-18; I John 3:16; Phil. 1:20; Eph. 6:18; Heb. 5:14).

3. Which principles of follow-up do you find in Acts 2:42-47?

Questions for Meditation and Application

1. How long should a new Christian remain a babe in Christ?

2. What have you done personally to help someone grow up?

3. Of the four areas of responsibility of a spiritual parent, pick at least two and prayerfully relate them to your work with people in the church. What will you do this week to strengthen this area of ministry?

CHAPTER 3

How to Follow Up

The early Christians reached their pagan world with the gospel within thirty-two years after the resurrection of Jesus Christ — without radio, printing press, or other mass media which are used to further the gospel in our day. How was it done?

In those days, witnessing believers were the rule instead of the exception. They seem to have been a special kind of Spirit-dominated men, with something in their lives which evidently is lacking today. Perhaps it was the personal touch of discipling and training that made such spiritual giants. Four different methods of follow-up on a personal level are demonstrated in the New Testament: personal contact, personal prayer, personal representatives, and personal correspondence.

Personal Contact

The Lord Jesus Christ and the Apostle Paul are the major examples of the first kind of follow-up. A number of times it is recorded that Jesus spoke in parables so that the multitude could not understand Him. No pastor today knowingly speaks above the heads of his people. Could it be that the Master was not primarily seeking to get His message across to the masses who listened to Him? His primary task was twofold: He came to seek and to save the lost by dying for our sins, and He went about for three years training a band of men who would give witness to His life, death, and resurrection. The cross, in God's plan, came only after His Son had prepared men to proclaim its good news of salvation. Jesus knew that His exemplary life before His disciples was as important to them as His words.

There is always a close relationship between one's life and speech when winning and building men for God. The Apostle John summarized this relationship as that "which we have heard, which we have seen with our eyes . . . and our hands have handled, of the Word of Life" (I John 1:1). By daily contact the Lord Jesus knew His disciples: He knew their needs and their desires, their weaknesses and their strong points. This close contact with men to train them for evangelism and follow-up might be called the "with him" principle.

Whom did the Master choose to be "with him?" "He called unto him his disciples: and of them he chose twelve, whom also he named apostles" (Luke 6:13). He had many followers and disciples, but of them He chose twelve to be apostles. Let us notice why: "that they should be with him, and that he might send them forth to preach" (Mark 3:14). He had two reasons for this personal contact: He wanted to share His life, and He wanted to share His ministry.

As the Lord Jesus Christ discipled men personally, so in our total ministry there must also be true discipling. To disciple a man is to lead him to experience Jesus as Lord of all his life. Being a disciple involves an act of surrender and a process of obedience. As a man continues in His word . . . glorifying the Father in bearing much fruit, so shall he be His disciple (John 8:31, 15:8).

This "with him" principle was also a dominant aspect of Paul's ministry. In Acts 20:4 there is a list of seven men who traveled with Paul and whom he taught the mysteries of the Christian life. Paul obviously loved personal contact with other believers. To the church at Rome he wrote of his desire to see them that they might be stabilized in the faith, and in Romans 16 he mentioned by name some thirty individuals in whom he was personally interested. To the Thessalonians he wrote, "Night and day praying exceedingly that we might see your face, and might perfect that which is lacking in your faith" (I Thess. 3:10).

A striking example of the driving passion of Paul for follow-up contact is recorded in Acts 14. As persecution developed at Antioch and Iconium, Paul's group was forced to flee. Arriving at Lystra, they healed an impotent man and were received as gods. They preached Christ, but soon Jews came from Antioch and Iconium and so agitated the people that they stoned Paul and left him for dead. Miraculously, he recovered and was spirited on to Derbe. Paul could have gone directly south to the coast and taken a ship for home. Instead, he returned northward to the cities where he had been threatened, persecuted, and stoned. His purpose was to see again those believers he had been forced to leave behind in the wake of persecution at Antioch, Iconium and Lystra, "strengthening the souls of the disciples, exhorting them to continue in the faith" (Acts 14:22). Paul placed his life in double jeopardy for the sake of this personal contact. His prime reason for living was follow-up (Phil. 1:23-25).

Just as the Lord and Paul found it necessary to spend time with their disciples, so we must project our lives and ministry into the lives of others. Casual social contact during church functions is insufficient to make a strong impact. Church leaders who take time to train individuals participate in building for eternity. Suggestions for spending personal time with another Christian for follow-up are listed in Chapter 5.

Just as Jesus "fed the multitudes" so there is also a large area of opportunity for mass follow-up in helping people grow into Christlikeness. But we must see the mass from the viewpoint of individual need. The Sunday School and Training Union[1] have proved to be effective organizations for group education and training. Later on we will describe new-member and personal-evangelism classes which are designed for use either with an individual or with a group. Often individual follow-up is attempted in a class situation, but a class will

[1] The Training Union is a member-building organization of the Southern Baptist Convention, meeting each Sunday evening before the services to instruct and train believers in Christian growth and practical service.

never substitute for the personal contact needed in building disciples to evangelize the world.

Personal Prayer

Both the Lord Jesus and Paul spent much time in intercession for new believers. The Master prayed all night before calling the twelve to be His disciples. For Peter He prayed that his faith fail not. The Lord knew how constant would be Satan's attacks on the faith of new believers. The protection of His disciples in His absence was the burden of His prayer on the night before His crucifixion. Paul began many of his epistles by referring to his constant, habitual intercession for new believers, that they might be conformed to the image of Christ and be filled with the knowledge of His will. The evangelistic movement which surged through the Roman provinces was the result of his continual prayer for the new believers. Prayer was one of his basic tools for follow-up.

To bring this mighty principle of personal prayer into the local church, each pastor must set the pace. Only as he spends time in daily intercession will he have a praying church. When his prayer life is what God would have it to be, he will be ready to follow any prompting from God to invite some layman into his study and teach him by example how to prevail in prayer. A book on prayer such a person might lay down and forget, but a close look into his pastor's heart in an hour of intercession for new converts, the church, and the world, is inescapably impressive and convincing.

The pastor may also teach intercession through the prayer meeting. If our Lord had to pray for Peter, a man who was with Him twenty-four hours a day, how much more need each pastor and church to cry out to God for the new believers in their midst. Christians do not automatically know the secrets of prayer — they must be taught.

Some churches have a prayer service and then a Bible teaching hour at the midweek meeting. A minimum of fifteen to thirty minutes should be used for prayer. The members could be divided into small groups of men, women, and young people, each group with a leader. Some of the leaders would probably be men trained individually in the pastor's study. An additional sheet of church-wide prayer requests in the Sunday bulletin could be handed out at prayer meeting and each group be asked to pray through the prayer list. Prayer requests should include the names of new Christians and new members, those who are sick, those who are bereaved, and the church staff and missionaries. There should also be prayers for the unsaved, for the laborers in evangelism, and for denominational needs. Encourage specific prayers in expectation of specific answers. Whatever methods are successful in bringing your church to its knees are valuable, as long as the church will follow up its new converts and membership by effective prayer. If a man is interceding, he *will* follow up.

Personal Representatives

When Paul was unable to visit the churches, he sent another man. In Philippians 2:19-22 he outlined some of his reasons for doing so and some of the qualifications for such a messenger. The Philippians were a joyful burden to Paul: "But I trust in the Lord Jesus to send Timotheus shortly unto you, that I also may be of good comfort, when I know your state. For I have no man likeminded, who will naturally care for your state" (Phil. 2:19-20). He was anxious to know the spiritual condition of the church at Philippi. But, being imprisoned in Rome, he was unable to go himself. What more normal thing than for him to send a man who had caught his own heart's vision to care for the Philippian converts?

There were not many men like Timothy, however: "For all seek their own, not the things which are Jesus Christ's" (2:21). Paul had trained this man to do what he would do in the same situation. How? "But ye know the proof of him, that, as a son with the father, he hath served with me in the gospel" (2:22). Being "with him" was Paul's method to prepare a person for personal work. Paul made it a habit to send his discipled men on missions of follow-up. Epaphroditus, Tychicus, and Titus also ministered on behalf of Paul to the believers in different churches. He sent out these trained men not only for follow-up, but also for communication between him and the churches.

Here is a scriptural pattern for follow-up work among the hundreds whom the pastor cannot personally contact. Sending a man is the basic idea of church visitation. Trained visitors, however, are rare. The pastor can multiply his outreach and his time for ministering when he trains laymen to visit. Such laymen should be able to handle even the most delicate spiritual situation. They must be trained to lead a soul to Christ, to counsel new believers, or to meet spiritual needs with the Word of God. Personal representatives are a projection of the pastor to the people, and a reflection of the church to the pastor.

Personal Correspondence

Much of the New Testament consists of letters to new believers, to encourage, teach, and guide them in their new faith. It was no accident that an imprisoned Paul wrote letters. His circumstances as well as his desire to help new believers kept him perpetually committed to contact through follow-up correspondence.

The five letters written by Peter and John indicate that they also realized the need for helping believers grow in grace. Peter records his reasons for writing in II Peter 1:12-15: "Wherefore I will not be negligent to put you always in *remembrance* of these things, though ye know them, and be established in the present truth. Yea, I think it meet ... to stir you up by putting you in *remembrance.* ... Moreover I will endeavour that ye may be able after my decease to have these things always in *remembrance.*" He wrote to refresh their memory, to stir them up, and to keep them remembering after his death. In the last twilight of his ministry, Peter was still burdened to follow up those people to whom he had previously ministered.

Luke's interest in follow-up was undoubtedly kindled by Paul. As they traveled together, Luke saw in many lives the effectiveness of Paul's follow-up correspondence. Luke addressed both his Gospel and The Acts to follow up one man, his friend Theophilus: "In order, most excellent Theophilus, that thou mightest know the certainty of those things, wherein thou hast been instructed" (Luke 1:3, 4). God used Paul, John, Peter, and Luke to build lives through their New Testament epistles.

Correspondence is a most fruitful avenue for follow-up today. It is the custom of most alert pastors to send a form letter or card to all who sign visitors' cards. Church visitors receive such an array of correspondence as picture postcards, church bulletins, questionnaires, thank-you notes, and doctrinal statements. This is a step in the right direction. But the power of the New Testament writers in correspondence was the power of the Word of God. The letters we write must be bathed in Scripture and lead the reader to the Christ of the Scriptures. They should encourage the application of Bible truths to life, because God promises to bless His Word.

Bible studies as enclosures in follow-up letters are being used by a number of churches and mission boards. The Billy Graham Team's follow-up office includes a simple Bible study with a letter of encouragement to those who make decisions in their meetings. A series of six simple lessons from John's Gospel are given in Appendix A as an aid to follow-up correspondence from the church.

A letter can also be a door-opener for further contact. A series of form letters on key Bible subjects sent conscientiously to unsaved visitors, the unenlisted, or to new believers is a device now being used with success by several churches. After visitation a brief, friendly, handwritten form letter may keep the door open for another visit.

Another way in which churches find it profitable to use the follow-up letter is to maintain close ties with students and service personnel away from home. A letter is a simple way to show them that their church at home continues to be interested in sharing with them the grace of God. They appreciate letters with enclosures of bulletins, printed sermons, Bible studies, and denominational literature.

Developing and sending out Scripture-filled letters demands a price in money, time, prayer, and discipline, but the results are eternal and this cannot be overemphasized. What a privilege has been given the earnest disciple who desires to follow-up through letter writing!

Two other aids to follow-up are the telephone and the tape recorder. Counsel, encouragement, and instruction may be easily given and prayer offered over the telephone when circumstances prohibit face-to-face fellowship. New believers will also be encouraged by messages, sermons, and personal words on tape. With this convenient aid, contact can be maintained and spiritual food given to the growing believer.

Questions to Answer

1. What are the four avenues of New Testament follow-up?
2. What is one reason for Luke's Gospel? (Luke 1:1-4).
3. What are three characteristics of a disciple? (John 8:31; 15:8; 13:34, 35).
4. What did Paul consider his main task on earth? (Phil. 1:23-25).

Questions for Meditation and Application

1. Of the four avenues of follow-up, which one reveals the greatest weakness in your follow-up program at church?
2. What is the best way to teach people to pray?
3. Ask God in prayer for two laymen you can adopt and disciple for Christ this year.

CHAPTER 4

The Pastor's Personal Preparation

To fulfill the great commission given by our Lord, to reach the world for Him, the pastor must lead his church to begin this task in its own community, city, and state. If we cannot get the message of salvation to everyone where we live, it is scarcely possible that we shall ever get it to the millions whose languages are unfamiliar and whose governments are antagonistic to Christianity.

Whatever the need in the local church, at the heart of its solution is the pastor. His life and ministry are clearly outlined in the book of Acts and the writings of Paul and Peter. The pastor should live on the Word and in prayer, and should minister as a discipler of men and as a leader in the church to the glory of God. He must hold tenaciously to this scriptural image of himself in the midst of the crushing pressures which tempt him to try to do everything and be everywhere.

His Devotional Life

The pastor must be an eyewitness of the living Christ through his face-to-face encounter and fellowship with Him in the Word. What he is before men is a reflection of what he is with his Saviour. The pastor, above all, has to resist the continual pressure to *do* rather than to study and pray; the "quiet time" must therefore have top priority each day. This quiet time is not sermon-building time, but heart-building time, a time for fellowship with Christ. The quiet time should never be hurried. It takes time to learn to walk with the Lord in prayer and in the Word. Rushing into and out of God's presence keeps modern men from securing the blessing which Moses received. To that humble man who tarried in intercession God replied, "My presence shall go with thee, and I will give thee rest" (Exod. 33:14). To be about our Father's business we must daily seek His presence and plan.

A pastor friend of mine was at the point of quitting the ministry altogether because there had been little fruit and much dissatisfaction in his church. On the advice of an older minister, he set aside the two hours from six to eight o'clock every morning for the purpose of reading the Bible and interceding for every member of his church. He found over a period of time that he averaged reading ten chapters daily on his knees, and he had time to approach the throne of grace boldly in specific prayer. Then he covenanted before God to fill every message with Scripture.

God began to save souls in that church; revival swept worldliness and spiritual lethargy from the congregation. Soon dozens of laymen were out preaching every week at thirty points in that city. Their missionary budget rose from $7,000 to $100,000 yearly in a period of eight years. This renewed pastor began to receive calls from around the world to teach missionaries and other ministers from the Word of God. "It all started," he said, "when I began to cry out to God and refused to leave my study until I had met God and knew His will for my daily schedule." This pastor's quiet time changed his life, his church, and then lives around the world.

His Example

The pastor must be an example; he must set the pace. His devotional life is revealed in the flow of his daily life. Throughout the history of the church, weakness in the pew has always been a reflection of some weakness in the pulpit. And back of the pulpit is the daily life of the pastor. Likewise, the major advances in the church have come through the leadership of the pulpit, backed up by a life of devotion to God. The calling of the pastor is primarily unto Christlikeness, to a life of holy living. A holy life radiates Christ and thus God is proclaimed through the pastor's life as well as through his speech.

Alexander McLaren said, "It isn't the much that you say you possess that shapes your character, but the little that you habitually live." More important than any sermon you will ever preach is your walk with God. We must be the embodiment of our message to others. We have been called to disciple men, but it takes a disciple to make a disciple, and our lives must be worth being copied. Jesus didn't say, *"Listen to Me* and I will make you fishers of men"; He said, *"Follow Me!"*

In writing to the church at Corinth, Paul twice commanded them, "Be ye followers of me" (I Cor. 4:16; 11:1). Writing to the Philippians, he exhorted them, "Be followers together of me, and mark them which walk so as ye have us for an ensample" (Phil. 3:17); and counseled them further, "Those things, which ye have both learned, and received, and heard, and seen in me, do: and the God of peace shall be with you" (4:9). By commanding the Thessalonians to follow his example, he emphasized that living the Christian life is a primary method of teaching doctrine. To Timothy and Titus he outlined the necessity of being an example, "In all things shewing thyself a pattern of good works" (Tit. 2:7).

Peter, in expounding the pastor's position, said, "Neither as being lords over God's heritage, but being ensamples to the flock" (I Pet. 5:3). The pastor's relationship to the church is horizontal, not vertical: he is to walk ahead of them, not reign over them. He walks ahead because he has gone farther with Christ in applying Scripture to life's experiences. And a pace-setter does not look over his shoulder to see who is following him so much as he looks to his goal — unto Jesus, his great Example.

His Ministry

The Bible reveals the pastor as a many-sided man. Apart from any natural talents, he must have the gift of pastoring, sovereignly bestowed by the Holy Spirit. In his calling as a pastor, the man becomes at the same time a teacher, a preacher, an overseer, a shepherd, and a parent. His life in Christ determines the emphasis and content of his varied ministries.

The Pastor as Teacher

A pastor has the duty of teaching. A teacher prepares and explains lessons to be taken home, but telling isn't always teaching. Sometimes a skill can be taught better by demonstration than by explanation. Church members are taught soul-winning by witnessing *with* them, not by just telling them to witness.

In Ephesians 4:11-12 the double gift of a pastor-teacher is given by the Spirit to perfect the saints to do the work of the ministry. The root word for "perfecting" in this passage is the same one used in the Gospels with reference to the disciples mending their nets. Many fishermen-pastors do much of their soul-winning one fish at a time. But this should not be their main job. God says they are to mend and unite the net of the body of Christ so that it catches many souls. Without an effective teaching ministry from the pastor, the members will never bring in nets filled to overflowing.

Listening is not necessarily learning. A well-filled church does not ensure a well-taught membership. Of the approximately one hundred to one hundred fifty sermons an active church member hears every year, most cannot remember five — perhaps not even the one heard last Sunday. Most of them do not even know that they are supposed to remember. If note-taking during the sermons is encouraged, the congregation will be better able to remember, use, and pass on what they have heard. A helpful sermon note guide is found in Appendix A.

The Pastor as Preacher

A sermon is like a fuse; it can set off dynamite or it can just sputter out and die in the pulpit. Its power or poverty usually rests with the pastor, depending on whether he is filled with the Holy Spirit and the Word of God or not. The pastor was, according to Luther and Calvin, a minister of the Word of God, a messenger transmitting God's Word to men. Many pastors of our nation have abandoned Bible banquets for spiritual tidbits and appetizers. They have become tinkling cymbals instead of His mighty messengers.

> So it was with G. Campbell Morgan. It was his habit to pass a short time in the loneliness of his study at the end of the day and while sitting in contemplation the strange question came to him, "Are you going to be a preacher or My messenger?" Then, says Dr. Morgan, "I began to look over my ministry, over the sermon I had just preached, and I discovered that subtly creeping into my life was the ambition to be a preacher. Then there came the spiritual struggle, and it was not until the grey light of dawn that the answer was given, 'I will be Your messenger.' "[1]

To be God's messenger, the preacher must fill his sermon with God's Word. God has given His Word as the tool for changing lives through the centuries. "The pastor's fundamental task in preaching is not to be clever or sermonic or profound, but to minister the truth of God," says Bernard Ramm. "If he is a true minister of God he is bound to the ministry of the Word of God."[2] Of the many types of sermons, the expository message inherently contains the most Scripture. Expository sermons encourage the congregation to follow the Scripture diligently as it is expounded. God always uses Bible-filled preaching to recruit disciples for lay evangelism and follow-up. Those caught by God with the Word will be the men who need to be followed up.

The Pastor as Overseer

An "overseer" is defined as a "superintendent" in *Thayer's Greek Lexicon*. The word for "overseer" is also translated as "bishop." The pastor or bishop has been called by God to oversee the work in His church. He is the "shop superintendent." A superintendent does not do the work; his task is

---

[1] G. H. Morling, *The Quest for Serenity*, p. 43.
[2] Bernard Ramm, *Protestant Biblical Interpretation*, p. 176

to co-ordinate and direct the workers in production and to counsel, correct, and guide them in difficulties. He is a production manager rather than a production worker. He is skilled, however, in all phases of the shop's work and can teach the worker any job.

Too many pastor-superintendents have been pressured by their churches into doing the "shop" work. According to A. E. Kernaban, "we have had too many spiritual tragedies where congregations have attempted to place the entire responsibility for the saving of their constituency upon the heart of their pastor or someone else brought in from the outside."[3] The pastor-superintendent is required to do the work of ten men to keep up the local church. It is good to have a man who can do the work of ten men — provided he is not the "shop superintendent" whose major job is to keep ten men producing.

If the pastor-superintendent does most of the work, then he does not have time for private devotions or for discipling men. He does not have time for training the workers who can boost production. One hard-working Southern pastor said to me, "You know, I simply can't meet with men personally; I don't have time." I am sure he didn't have time; and he never will, unless he makes it, unless he catches the vision of what it means to train men to be faithful workers and soul-winners.

A scriptural overseer is no accident. A man who has time to pray, to plan, and to prepare his heart in the Word must either have a large paid staff to do the work or else train enough laymen for leadership responsibilities. The best foremen are those trained personally by the superintendent. They know what he wants, how he thinks, and what his plans are for production. These things are learned most thoroughly and most quickly when they are learned man-to-man from the superintendent.

According to Paul, the duty of an overseer is to feed and protect his flock (Acts 20:20-32). He went from house to house teaching and warning the believers in Ephesus (Acts 20:20).

[3] A. E. Kernaban, *Visitation Evangelism*, p. 38

"So ever be on your guard and always remember that for three years, night and day, I never ceased warning you one by one, and that with tears" (Acts 20:31, Williams). When Paul left Ephesus, he had trained overseers to care for the flock. What pastor today would feel free to be gone an extended period of time and turn his congregation over to the preaching and teaching ministry of a few men in the church? In the short period of three years, Paul could leave the church to his trained overseers, commending them to God and to the Word of His grace.

The Pastor as Shepherd

"Shepherd" and "pastor" have been used synonymously since Old Testament times. The pastor must have a shepherd-heart, instinctively caring for his charge, just as a shepherd knows, and watches over, his sheep with loving concern. The shepherd's job is a demanding one: he leads his sheep, keeps them from harm, and guides them to green pastures.

> Shepherding is never spectacular. It is humble work. A man has to come down from the stilts of his self-importance to do it. In this sense, every good shepherd gives his life for the sheep. Place, position, prestige, and personal comfort are not the considerations when one is called to shepherd the flock. The comfort and care of the people become the burden of the true pastor.[4]

The shepherd knows his sheep, as the Good Shepherd said, "I . . . know my sheep, and am known of mine" (John 10:14). Standing behind the pulpit will not give the pastor a real knowledge of his flock. He must spend much time with the sheep. In Exodus 28:12 and 29 Aaron, the high priest, was commanded to bear upon the breastplate over his heart the names of the children of Israel and to go into the holy place for communion and intercession. As Aaron took the names of the people to God, so the pastor-shepherd must take the needs and burdens of his sheep into the presence of the Lord.

[4] R. A. Anderson, *The Shepherd—Evangelist*, p. 557.

So in order to pray for each one properly and individually, he must know them.

The shepherd also leads his sheep: "And when he putteth forth his own sheep, he goeth before them" (John 10:4). A pastor is a leader because he is "out in front," setting the pace spiritually. He has been placed there by the Holy Spirit. His is a leadership by the grace of God and is not accomplished or merited by the man himself. The pastor, therefore, is never above anyone, but, rather, he is a servant of all. Whenever the shepherd ceases to "go before the sheep," he ceases to be a true shepherd because the true shepherd always leads, choosing the "paths of righteousness" for his sheep.

The Pastor as Parent

The pastor is not only a shepherd but a spiritual foster parent. He has a special relationship with and responsibility for his church that can best be likened to those of a parent. In I Corinthians 4:15 Paul reminded the believers at Corinth of his unique relationship with them; he was their father whom God used to help bring them to new life in Christ. And writing to the Thessalonian believers (I Thess. 2:7) he compared himself to a nursing mother. In verse eleven he called himself a father to them. As a father he "exhorted and comforted and charged every one . . . as a father doth his children." As their spiritual father God used him to bring children to maturity and fruitful reproduction.

Every person who is born into the kingdom of God is born a babe in Christ. There is no hurry-up process for making men out of babies; it takes time, expense, and sacrifice on the part of parents. Regardless of age, wealth, education, or position, all new Christians are babies and need parental care. Babies are the most demanding beings on earth, not only because of their natural helplessness and inability to reason, but also because of their self-centeredness. Only the mature person is capable of living for others.

With this perspective, the wise pastor will not delegate

adult jobs in the church to spiritual babies, regardless of their social status or reputation. He will not place babies in charge of other babies, or use them to teach adults. He must give new converts special training and care, feeding them a selected spiritual diet, so that with growth they may become responsible for the care and feeding of others new in Christ.

All parents have a fourfold responsibility in bringing their children to maturity: they are to love, to feed, to protect, and to train them (cf. Chapter 2). A baby cannot be loved too much with the kind of love defined in I Corinthians 13. Paul said, "So being affectionately desirous of you, we were willing to have imparted unto you, not the gospel of God only, but also our own souls, because ye were dear unto us" (I Thess. 2:8). Such love for spiritual children engendered a mature church.

A parent must also feed his children the milk and meat of the Word of God. Though he does not always do all the feeding, it is his responsibility to see that it is done. The pastor is responsible for feeding his church the Word through his messages, and for the content of all literature used in the church. Children need food every day; and so do spiritual babes. Since the pastor can serve the congregation usually only two or three well-prepared sermons a week, he must teach his charges to eat daily by themselves at home.

Children must also be protected and corrected through doctrinal preaching, teaching, and firm exhortation, so that they may be prepared against Satan's attacks in the form of personal temptations, unbalanced splinter groups, and unwholesome cults.

A spiritual child is trained in the expected essentials of eating (the Word), talking (prayer), walking (obedience), and sharing (witnessing). These performances are not inculcated automatically into the spiritual life by mere church attendance; they are best learned from an experienced spiritual parent.

The pastor connot be a parent for every new believer, but

he can be the example of a spiritual parent to the whole church. It is his responsibility to see that each child in the faith is cared for by someone. And where does he find parent-hearted disciples equipped to follow-up the babes in Christ? Among those he has already trained and followed up himself, man-to-man, who have learned from his own parent-heart how to help new believers grow to maturity.

Growing believers eventually make mature, Christlike disciples. With careful parental care, these maturing Christians will soon see the need to love, feed, protect, and train others. They *do* unto others what others have *done* unto them! As the vision grows, God will give the church many spiritually responsible foster parents who will care for those won to Christ. The parent-heart is duplicated in future parents as spiritual children are raised up to full spiritual stature and Christlikeness.

Questions to Answer

1. What qualifications did Peter set forth for a minister? (I Pet. 5:1-3).
2. Is it scriptural for men to follow men? (I Cor. 4:16; Phil. 4:9).
3. What are five facets of a pastor's ministry to others?

Questions for Meditation and Application

1. How can you make your own "quiet time" more practical?
2. How disciplined a pace are you willing to set to make disciples in your church who will assuredly reproduce?
3. What is the best way to build a church of parent-hearted members? (Phil. 2:19-23).
4. Consider what you can do now to enlist the membership in your church in taking notes on your sermons.
5. Have you found a good method of Bible study you can teach to your laymen? (Note Appendix A suggestions).

CHAPTER 5

Building Spiritually Qualified Laymen

"Preachers are not sermon makers, but men makers and saint makers,"[1] says E. M. Bounds. But is this true today? So often the demands of the church hinder the discipling of the individual. The press of time favors group meetings rather than personal training. However, discipling the individual is God's way of producing the needed teachers, leaders, and soul-winners. To reach the mass we must reach the individual.

It takes time to build men, but this long-range vision will ensure a fruitful and mature church. Following up individuals *now* will provide quality leadership in the years to come. If follow-up is not a priority task in the pastor's program he will always be short on men who can teach, visit, and win others to Christ and the church. What we promote and pursue in the present will determine what the church is going to be in the future.

Although Jesus ministered to thousands, it was to a special group of disciples, the Twelve, that He gave most of His time, teaching them and training them. Almost everything the Lord did or said was in the context of this training and discipling. He was not primarily interested in healing, although His ministry is dotted with instances when He made people whole in body and in spirit. Neither was He an intellectual, engaged in philosophical or theological hair-splitting and advancing ideas to elevate the minds of men. Nor was He primarily a social reformer, for He taught men to be obedient to the existing ruling power.

[1] E. M. Bounds, *The Preacher and Prayer,* p. 10.

Jesus Christ was essentially a teacher, and therefore a discipler of men. He used preaching, healing, and discussion to stimulate, startle, and awaken. These were His tools for training the band of men who were to take the message of salvation, the message of His life, death and resurrection, around the world.

Results of Discipling Men

That peer of pulpit giants, Charles Haddon Spurgeon, prayed, "Lord, give me twelve men who love souls and I'll shake London from end to end!" He didn't have the twelve at that time, but God heard his prayer, and before long young men were being trained to win souls. In a few years, London was shaken with the gospel message as never before by this man and his helpers.

Early in his ministry, a prominent pastor preached a fiery message on soul-winning, then called the church to visitation. Only three were there at the specified time: the minister, his wife, and the janitor. Disheartened, the pastor drove to the home of a deacon and talked him into going out for just two visits. On the second call they led a person to Christ. Later the deacon asked if he might go with the pastor again the next week.

After three months of witnessing experience with his pastor, the deacon won his first man to Christ and began to take him along as he sought to reach others. In two years one hundred sixty-nine people were led to the Lord and became active in that church. Most of them were won by recent converts who had been trained man-to-man.

One who originally helped to develop the follow-up techniques used in the Billy Graham Crusades was Lorne Sanny, General Director of The Navigators. Lunching with a young pastor he had known in a previous campaign, Sanny began to question him and his four laymen guests about their church. One of the laymen related the fact that they had received eight hundred fifty additions to their church on profession of faith in the two years since the Crusade.

"How did that come about?" asked Sanny.

The pastor recalled their conversation two years before when Sanny had challenged him to train a man. At that time he had one layman open to learn, willing to work, and hungry to help others to learn to know Christ. The pastor had taken this man with him everywhere. Through that one layman he now had sixty-two persons growing in discipleship, men who were witnessing consistently and bringing those won into the church.

Heart Census for Pastors

"How many *new* soul-winners and soul-builders do you have in your church this year you didn't have twelve months ago?" was a question put to a pastors' conference recently by a member of the Billy Graham team.[2] The answer to that question provides a reasonably accurate evaluation of the pastor's personal interest in following up men. One pulpiteer admitted, "I preach to seventeen hundred people on Sunday mornings; I think I have three who know *how* to lead a person to Christ and do it!"

In seeking qualified counselors to do a simple soul-winning task in a Western Graham Crusade, the team had four thousand people who applied and attended soul-winning classes. Out of that number, twenty-four hundred qualified as being able to lead a soul to Christ, personally. But they represented some twelve hundred co-operating churches — an average of only two qualified personal workers per church! Many churches didn't qualify any counselors at all.

Our primary job as pastor is the perennial development of a corps of lay soul-winners and workers. But how can we best do that? Class work alone, especially on a "take it or leave it" basis, will never adequately substitute for that personal time

[2] W. B. Moore, "Evangelism in Depth," *The Baptist Standard*, March 1960, p. 7.

given a few men each week, teaching them the basics of the Christian life. The pastor must re-evaluate his ministry in terms of the individual; he must concentrate his efforts on men to get workers. For example, if every pastor or church leader in the Southern Baptist Convention discipled one layman per year until he had learned to win and care for a soul, there would be almost thirty thousand *new* soul-winners each year!

Samuel Shoemaker puts it like this: "It is not the main job of the church to turn out a lot of work, list a long string of members, or raise a lot of money. It is the main job of the church to fashion people who behave like Jesus Christ. They cannot be hewn out of the mediocre mass wholesale, but only one by one."[3]

Selecting a Man

There are three groups of individuals in the church competing for the pastor's time: the leaders and potential leaders, the enlisted, and the unenlisted members. The public ministry of the pastor will be his chief contact with the two latter groups. Their further care will come through the regular church organizations and the lay leadership trained by the pastor. It is on the leader and potential-leader groups that the pastor can most profitably concentrate his individual ministry.

To begin with, the pastor faces this important question: Should he adopt an older Christian leader in the church or start discipling a new convert or younger layman who is a potential leader? The answer depends on the pastor and the layman involved. As a general rule, men recently converted are more teachable and more open to their pastor's suggestions. The eighteen-to-forty age group is usually considered stable, yet flexible and receptive to new ideas.

Any man chosen to be discipled must prove himself faithful

[3] Samuel M. Shoemaker, *Revive Thy Church Beginning With Me*, p. 112.

and be able to teach others what the pastor teaches him. He must be responsive, correctable, and available to the pastor. Normally a deacon or a Sunday-school teacher should be chosen. Before choosing a man to disciple, the pastor should spend much time in prayer and meditation on this important step. Our Lord prayed all night before choosing twelve from the hundreds who followed after Him. Since the pastor's time is so valuable, he must be led by the Spirit to choose a man who will reproduce this personal training into other lives.

But you may ask, "Wouldn't this emphasis on one or two men cause problems of jealousy and division in the Church?" Not necessarily. Is it scriptural for a pastor to "specialize" on a few men for the purpose of training? The Lord Jesus and the Apostle Paul did. The pastor can answer any criticism that he is spending too much time with selected people by giving a general church invitation for every man willing to begin personal Bible study, intercession for the lost, and house-to-house evangelism to meet him at the church at a specified time. If more than one or two respond, he may use this group as a nucleus for this first New Members Class or Adoption Plan. Then he can choose the most faithful of them for personal training. With an open invitation he can silence criticism.

Another question that has been raised is, "Will this emphasis on man-to-man training create the problem of making people pastor-centered?" It is true that many churches have fallen apart when their pastor left because of too strong an attachment to him, but the man-to-man ministry of a pastor has the opposite effect. Congregations usually become pastor-centered when they are not feeding on the Word of God for themselves. A pastor who is working with individuals teaches each man to feed himself on the Word and to have his daily "quiet time." Thus men become Christ-centered through the Word and prayer, and not pastor-dependent through lack of it.

Perhaps the most serious hindrance to individual discipling is the pastor's cry of not having enough time. This problem should be brought before God in prayer. It is a matter of vision rather than of lack of time. We make time to do what we consider most essential. We will never be more "about the Father's business" than was Jesus. For three years He took time, while ministering to the masses, to disciple and train twelve men. If we seek to have His vision, we will make time also for the discipling of one or two men each year.

Ways of Sharing the Life

After selecting an individual to disciple, the pastor should begin to spend time with him. "Iron sharpeneth iron; so a man sharpeneth the countenance of his friend" (Prov. 27:17). The sharing of Christian life and experiences changes both people. Being "with him" is a prerequisite for sharpening a man.

In analyzing the work of our Lord, the Master Discipler of men, one expositor has carefully summarized His training methods as follows: The disciples lived with Jesus. Their number was small, which ensured personal, individual contact. They accompanied Him as He performed His tasks of teaching, preaching, and healing. They received doctrinal instruction in the context of its practical significance. It has further been said that Jesus' training of His men related to character and personality rather than to skill in the use of knowledge and method.

The disciples learned through observation how Jesus preached, healed, and taught. It is interesting to note that they never asked Him to teach them to preach or to heal, only to pray. The time Jesus spent in prayer with the Father was the only time He was hid from the searching eyes of His men. But can we have men live with us as He did? In many church situations this would be impossible. In some larger churches young seminary graduates or students are used as assistant pastors for a year or two. Few churches, however, can afford this expensive kind of man-to-man training. Developing a summer program for returned collegians is one method by which a pastor can disciple future missionaries and church leaders. A strong collegiate program during the summer months has greatly blessed the ministry of a large Western Presbyterian church; literally dozens of young men and women have gone out as pastors and missionaries as a result of this person-to-person program centered on evangelism and Bible study. Some parsonages are large enough for one or two selected young people to live with their pastor for a few weeks of more personalized home training.

But any pastor can take advantage of the opportunities to take a man with him as he travels, speaks, and visits. The "with him" contact is essential for getting to know each other. When a pastor asks a man to visit with him, he must have much more in mind than companionship while doing a church duty. Every contact with a layman is a training opportunity. As the layman shares his pastor's tasks, he learns to witness, to apply the Scriptures to actual situations and to have a pastor-heart for the church. Unless the "with him" principle is clearly in focus, our work with men will be hazy, dissipated, and non-productive.

Going with the disciple is another phase of man-to-man training. "He that had been possessed with the devil prayed him that he might be with him. Howbeit Jesus *suffered him not*" (Mark 5:18-19). Although the Lord was constantly accompanied by the twelve, there were many others, such as this man, who were sent home to witness where they lived. To reach the area of the church's influence with the gospel, we must also work with other men in *their* area of influence. If the pastor takes a layman or convert away from the latter's contacts and friends, then the pastor's friends become the man's friends, and the pastor's circle his circle. The "church circle" can soon rob the layman of potential contacts.

To train a man for his sphere of influence means that we keep him where he is, unless his job is dishonoring God, and help him to witness there. His prime responsibility is to those among whom he lives and where he is known. "Go home to thy friends and tell them," Jesus said to a certain man. The better acquainted we are with the Christian worker's environment, the faster we will be able to help him meet his needs in disseminating the Word. In his own environment a man learns more easily; the Lord gets a witness in that particular sphere of influence, and the spiritual father thus expands his ministry to new people. All this results in multiplied church witness.

Openness before God and man is a mark of a true disciple. We are commanded to be "sincere" or "transparent" (Phil. 1:10). If you are willing to "give" yourself to laymen, you will find them in turn willing to share more of their heart secrets with you. Lack of openness with laymen is a great obstacle to getting to know their problems and needs. "As in water face answereth to face, so the heart of man to man." (Prov. 27:19). Laymen tend to put their pastors on a pedestal and such a compliment is pleasing to the flesh, but sooner or later they see us as we are, shorn of our pastoral "pre-eminence" and equally in need of God's grace. Being honest with men about ourselves keeps them looking to Christ and not to us.

When speaking to a group of new believers after a city-wide campaign, a minister shared with them the trouble he had in consistently setting apart a special time for daily prayer. They expressed real shock that an older Christian should experience one of their own struggles. For the first time they openly began to tell about their own failures in getting time alone with the Lord. By being honest, the minister was able to help them with a basic spiritual problem in their lives. This does not mean that we must display all our private sins. It does mean that we must be open to others by honestly admitting that we are not impervious to temptation. We share our total life with others as we spend time with them.

How to Disciple a Layman

Regular personal contact is necessary for discipling a man. The pastor should set aside at least one hour a week to meet with each layman he seeks to disciple. Different men have different needs and demand more or less time. Because of crowded schedules, most pastors find they have to plan ahead to *make time* for being with their men. Besides these regular hours we must also be available to our men at any hour of the day. They have their own "growing pains" and the problems of others to unburden.

The following simple instructions are practical for any teaching ministry:

Tell him why. A man must have the proper motivation for a task. Whether you assign him a certain project or a Bible lesson always tell him why. Answering the "Why should I?" in his mind is the first step toward a completed task.

Show him how. The life you live should be the best example of how the task can be done. Your man learns how to win a soul to Christ by watching you do it before he tries it himself. To start him on Bible study or Scripture memory, show him how you do it. Then ask him questions to see whether or not he understands.

Get him started. Outline a definite study or project for him to do before the next meeting. Give assignments that meet his spiritual needs. Start with small assignments which are gauged to his educational and spiritual level, and make sure that he understands, and agrees to complete all work. Never break his confidence by not expecting a good job; keep your training standards high. Suggest strongly that he begin work on his assignment immediately. The goal is to bring men to the place of decision and so build daily faithfulness in his life, not letting him get by with sporadic bursts of activity to complete a job. Increase assignments as you become more familiar with his individual pace.

Keep him going. Never give anyone a new task without checking at the next meeting to see if the previous one was done correctly. Checking up shows him you are interested in his spiritual progress. It will challenge him to improve and to succeed. Give him genuine encouragement, but guard against false praise: he knows what it really took for him to get that assignment done. Then require him to give a résumé of it. **This will show you what he has learned and what he doesn't** understand. If he can't give a concise résumé, he will not be **able to teach it to anyone else. Teach him to take notes;** he **can't remember the Scriptures and the assignments without** **jotting them down.**

Completed assignments are a realistic test of a man's faith- **fulness. If he fails in an assignment and excuses himself for** **lack of time, then phone him the next week and ask him how** he is doing — don't let him fail for lack of your checking up. If **he continues to do incomplete work, perhaps you have given** **him too much to do. Whenever he fails to do the work as-** **signed, always ask him why; he should not be allowed to con-** **tinue to fail. Sometimes you might resort to making your** **meeting date dependent upon his completion of an assign-** **ment. Tell him to call you when he is ready with it; if he fails** **to call, he will possibly always be an unfaithful disciple.**

Checking up is much the same as a school exam: after a **number of failures the student should be dropped from the** **class. God does not require you to spend your time with men** **who will not produce. They can be cared for in the normal** **church program. Prayerfully decide before the Lord how** **much further personal time you can give to such a man. Before** **dropping him, however, explain that the reason for spending** **your time together was for the purpose of his spiritual growth.** **Continue to indicate your love for him and your desire that** **he become mature. Tell him you are willing to meet with him** **whenever he wants personal help.**

Teach him to reproduce. **Continually put before the student** **the responsibility of sharing what he is learning with others.** **Give him an occasional assignment that must be passed on to** **someone else. Until he can give to others what you are giving** **to him, your training relationship is not yet productive. Ex-** **perience in helping others now will prepare him for a more** **fruitful personal ministry later on. By choosing a qualified** **Sunday-school teacher or deacon to start your man-to-man** training you facilitate a more rapid multiplication of Christ's personal ministry throughout the church organization.

Using the Bible to Meet Needs

Minister to your trainee from the Scriptures. Do not just answer his questions, but direct him to fitting Bible verses. When necessary, rebuke with the cutting edge of God's Word.

One West Coast pastor simply writes down the Bible references which answer the questions of his callers, and asks them to look them up for themselves and prayerfully find God's answer. This practice — with all its limitations — does get people to seek answers from God's viewpoint. It builds the habit of Bible-centered living.

Three Essentials

In I Thessalonians 2:11 Paul recalls how he "exhorted, comforted, and charged every one of you, as a father doth his children." To exhort, to comfort, and to charge gives proper balance to our instruction. The word "exhort" means "to call near" or "to encourage." It has the sense of urging someone to pursue a particular course of conduct.[4] We are to remind our student of what he probably knows already, but is not doing. Then we must point out the truths of God's Word and use them to rebuke and admonish him if discipline is needed.

To "comfort" is "to cheer or help." The emphasis in this context is on helping or stimulating a person to the energetic accomplishment of a particular job[5]. We accept his burdens and problems as our own, and pray with him about them. He must be encouraged to believe God in the midst of his problems. "Be Power conscious, not problem conscious" exclaimed a great missionary. Scriptural "comforting" motivates a person to a maximum life of faith.

The word "charge" means to "testify" or "to make known

---

4 Hogg and Vine, *The Epistles to the Thessalonians*, p. 66.
5 *Ibid.*

from experience."[6] This is the teaching-and-learning aspect of working with a man. A father must continually impart new truth to his child. If the student can be shown that the answer to his problems lies in his spiritual growth, then he will become interested in the Word and in prayer. We must choose basic spiritual food consistent with his present needs and interests.

I Thessalonians 2:11 encompasses a threefold responsibility — to remind strongly, to stimulate and help, and to "bear witness" or teach doctrine to our men from our own experience. The pastor exhorts, comforts, and charges his pupil according to the guidance of the Spirit and the needs of the moment.

The Importance of Goals

Christlikeness is the ultimate goal for a Christian. There must be more tangible intermediate goals, however, such as the application of God's Word to spiritual conditions, consistent and effectual prayer, obedience to the Lord's revealed will, and witnessing of His grace to others. Applying these basic principles produces maturity or Christlikeness. Our assignments must be designed to stimulate each Christian to grow continually in the grace and love of God. We should take an inventory of our pupil's progress toward these intermediate goals from time to time.

Just as Jesus looked beyond the apostles to the men they would reach and train (John 17:20), so we must envision our trainee's value to Christ and His church five, ten, twenty years from now. He should be shown how his life fits into God's divine plan for reaching the world. For instance, Genesis 22:18 records how one man's obedience changed the world. One of the greatest convictions we can ever impart to another is that God wants to use him. Other helps for building men are found in the Appendices.

[6] *Ibid.*

Teaching Doctrine

What would you teach a layman if you had his ear an hour a week for three months? An older minister responded to a similar query by saying that he would be at a loss to know where to start or what to teach. Would you enroll him in a three-month study course? If so, what course?

The material in the New Member Class (Appendix C) is especially helpful for laying a doctrinal foundation with an individual or with a group. The first thing to do to help a man is to meet his problems with the Word of God. The next task is to make up his most obvious deficiencies in the basics of Bible study, prayer, obedience, and witnessing (pp. 137ff.; 172ff.). Then the five ways to master the Word should be taught to every layman: how to hear, read, study, memorize, and meditate on the Scriptures (Appendix A). Each man must learn to walk in obedience and live the life of faith. He must be trained how to witness and how to care for those he wins to Christ.

All other teaching is dependent on these basics of Christian living. By knowing and exercising his spiritual gifts, a layman will realize his responsibility to the local church and support his ministry.

"But what can you give a man in just a few sessions?" you may ask, pastor. If you had but three meetings with a man, perhaps the most important things to teach him would be why and how we have a "quiet time" (pp. 182f.), why and how to memorize key Scripture verses (pp. 163ff.), and why and how to know God's will through daily guidance of the Spirit (pp. 183ff). A group of mature laymen will be the result if the pastor learns to work with men by first discipling a man!

Questions to Answer

1. What is the greatest joy a Christian may have in service? (III John 4).

2. What are the two standards of good follow-up in a church? (Phil. 2:15, 16; I Thess. 3:5).

3. Name the five steps in a practical teaching ministry with laymen.

Questions for Meditation and Application

1. What aspect of your ministry will give the church mature soul-winners?

2. Do you want any more soul-winners in your church next year than the past year? If you do, what must you stress differently in your own ministry?

3. Have you found at least one man in your church who meets the scriptural standards for man-to-man witnessing and is open to discipling?

4. Where in your weekly schedule can you plan time for this man?

CHAPTER 6

Follow Up and Multiply

Follow-up is the best way to bring the scriptural principle of multiplication back into the church. Once a new convert has been "brought up" spiritually and has won his first soul, the principle is at work. Building one life in Christ and continuing with that person until he in turn reaches and builds another who will reproduce is multiplication. This is the planned vision for reaching future generations through those we win now.

The Scriptures provide for a third and fourth generation of believers through spiritual parents. Ideally, of course, these were to be the natural parents; God's promises to bless the people of Isreal were predicated upon their obedience to His command to teach their children's children. In the context of the greatest command, "Thou shalt love the Lord thy God with all thine heart" (Deut. 6:5), is given the warning to "keep all his statutes and his commandments, which I command thee, thou, and thy son, and thy son's son, all the days of thy life" (v. 2). To receive the blessing of God the Israelites were to teach their children and their grandchildren His precepts.

Each new generation must face the command of Christ to take the gospel into all the world. Every generation is responsible for evangelizing its contemporaries. The Bible records the tremendous inroads the gospel made into the pagan world in the first century. Without printing press, automobiles, radio, or airplanes, those in the early church reached their world with the message of Christ. When the multiplication principle is applied, it is possible to evangelize the world in one generation.

The Imperative of Multiplication

Multiplication is God's plan to populate the world, both physically and spiritually. His first command given to man was to "be fruitful and multiply" (Gen. 1:28). Starting with two people, the earth now is bulging with over two and one-half billion souls. The "corruptible seed" has certainly multiplied. Christians are born, however, "not of corruptible seed, but of incorruptible, by the Word of God." If, therefore, "corruptible seed" can produce over two billion people, cannot the "incorruptible seed" of the Word of God do the same? Today there are millions more who have never heard the name of Christ than there were in the days of the Apostles. Multiplication is the plan of God for matching spiritual birth with population expansion.

It is obvious that addition can never reach the world for Christ. One hundred and fifty years ago the world's population was only half what it is today. It is multiplying at such a rate that in less than twenty-five years there will be over four billion people, almost double what there are now. Spiritually, addition has not and cannot ever keep pace.

Less than five percent of those in the church "add" by winning souls. They may win thousands throughout a denomination, but unless these who are won somehow win others also, in a few decades the number of believers will be swallowed up by the masses of the unsaved and unchurched. Our only hope for reaching the masses is by multiplication.

Here is how multiplication can work in the church, as described by a pioneer of this vision:

> Along with the believer's spiritual activity, he has the one desire to be a spiritual father. He is praying that God will give him a man. Perhaps it takes him six months to reach another for Christ and get him started giving out the Word, and getting a man for himself.
>
> So this first man at the end of the six months has another man. Each man wins another in the following six months. At the end of the year, there are just four of them ... The four get together, have prayer and determine not to allow anything to sidetrack them. They want to get the gospel

out to a lot of people, but check up on at least *one* and see him through.

So the four of them in the next six months each get a man. That makes eight at the end of a year and a half; at the end of two years there are sixteen. Three years produce sixty-four; at the end of five years there are 1,024. At the end of fifteen and a half years there are 2,176,000,000 won, the population of the world in persons over three years of age.[1]

The potential for multiplication through the church is phenomenal. To win and teach one man to reproduce every six months is not an unrealistic personal goal. Many Christian workers win more than one soul every six months. It is what *happens* to that one soul that makes the big difference between addition and multiplication of souls.

The Multiplication Principle in Scripture

Jesus knew that only through multiplication could the gospel be proclaimed to every creature. In the midst of the mass He concentrated on a personal ministry with the Twelve and for three years He prepared them for their ministry of multiplication. Through twelve men (the eleven and Paul) would come the first-generation thrust toward world evangelization. Jesus saw in these men "the foundations of many generations" (Isa. 58:12).

It was Andrew, one of the quiet disciples, whose ministry first multiplied into four "generations." Andrew found his brother, Simon, later called Peter, and brought him to Jesus. A Spirit-filled Peter preached at Pentecost, and three thousand were converted. These converts, nurtured at Jerusalem in the period between Acts 2 and 8, went out from there preaching the Word (Acts 8:4). Traveling to Antioch (Acts 11:19), these lay-witnesses won many to Christ. Then for at least a year Barnabas and Paul followed up these new converts at Antioch and a strong church was established there. This first "mission station" of the church was estab-

[1] Dawson Trotman, *Born to Reproduce*, p. 36.

lished through multiplication of Andrew's personal work years before. Andrew, Peter, the three thousand, and the church at Antioch made four "generations" of discipled converts.

Paul had the "fourth-generation" vision for reproducers. One illustration of his practical witnessing and follow-up is given in Acts 18. He had labored with Aquila and Priscilla, two other Jewish tentmakers whom he discipled in the Good News. After Paul left them, these two saw an opportunity to witness to Apollos, a brilliant orator from Alexandria who had come to Ephesus, and who knew the teaching of John the Baptist but was evidently uninformed about the resurrected Christ and the work of the Holy Spirit. Quickly the tentmakers "adopted" this young man and taught him the Word: "They took him unto them and expounded unto him the way of God more perfectly" (Acts 18:26). This couple unlocked their hearts and their knowledge of the Lord to this inadequately taught man.

The Scriptures further relate that Apollos "mightily convinced the Jews, and that publicly, showing *by the scriptures* that Jesus was Christ" (Acts 18:28). Apollos profited by that reflection of Paul's teaching which he had caught from Priscilla and Aquila and began to reproduce.[2] Men must be living in the Word before they can multiply their witness. Paul, Aquila and Priscilla, Apollos, the convinced Jews — four "generations" resulting from the teaching ministry of a man who always looked toward future generations while discipling men.

Paul said to Timothy (second "generation"), "And the things which thou hast heard of me among many witnesses, the same commit thou to faithful men [third "generation"], which shall be able to teach others also [fourth "generation"]" (II Tim. 2:2). The word "commit" is a strong imperative. We have no choice as to whether we follow up and

---

2 F. W. Farrar, *Life and Work of Paul*, p. 116.

multiply; we must be obedient "to the heavenly vision" as was Paul.

The principle of multiplication sets limits on the *kind* of men we concentrate on, so that the generations to come are reached. We must "deposit as a trust" what we have learned "to faithful men." To commit the Word to men, however, we should start with one faithful man. This man must be "able," or adequate for teaching others.

In itself, committing or depositing truth to men is not multiplication. Each must respond to the truth of the gospel by building others specifically with future generations in view. "Paul's idea of sharing the Gospel with oncoming generations is the very genius of Christianity," says O. R. Mangum. "God has no other plan. This is a debt our generation owes to the next. This is the only apostolic succession we find in scripture."[3]

Just as a chain is only as strong as its weakest link, a vision is only as strong as its weakest recipient. While a babe in Christ Paul could not have discipled Timothy or envisioned future generations through him. But as Paul grew toward maturity, his potential for winning and discipling men increased proportionately. Likewise, Timothy as a babe in Christ had to grow before he could multiply his ministry.

Areas of Weakness

Few converts ever reproduce, however, and the multiplication chain is broken after the second "generation." One reason the convert doesn't reproduce is that he doesn't want to. Or he may not have had follow-up care, and thus lacks the maturity for building others. The first "generation's" lack of vision for multiplication, however, is the most serious hindrance to a chain of four "generations." Vision for the fourth "generation" determines what is *done* for the second "generation."

[3] O. R. Mangum, *Paul's Swan Song*, pp. 45-46.

That multiplication is a church-wide need is evident. Where are the men in our churches who are going on for Christ, winning still others? One mission board leader, in questioning candidates for overseas services, found that less than five percent of them had won people to Christ who were growing and living victoriously. Of course, there are pastors and lay leaders who can point to their fourth "generation" without having had in focus the principle of multiplication. But there is no place for chance in building future Christian "generations" when God has given in His Word a dynamic principle for success in getting the gospel to every ear in our generation!

Essentials of Multiplication

There are certain basic "laws" that govern spiritual multiplication. First, there is the law of relationship. The more consistently we walk in the fullness of the Holy Spirit, keeping in close contact with Him through the Word and through prayer, the deeper will become our fellowship with Christ.

Jesus had broadening circles of personal contact with His disciples. In the Scriptures are listed the three, the twelve, the seventy, the one hundred and twenty, and the five hundred. Of the twelve, Peter, James and John had the most intimate fellowship with Christ. These of the inner circle eventually experienced the greatest revelation of Him. Paul, alone in the desert with the Lord for three years,[4] had the same amount of personal contact with the resurrected Son of God as did the others during the three years of His earthly ministry. Of the twenty-seven New Testament books, at least twenty came from these men — those closest to Christ were given His mightiest revelations.

We seek to bring those we disciple into the inner circle of fellowship with Christ. To reach a third and fourth "generation," we must attach our men firmly to Christ Him-

4 Farrar, *op. cit.*

self. We must set the pace in our devotion to the Lord so that men will have a path to follow.

Second, there is the law of commitment. A person must be committed to reaching future generations for Christ; his course of life must be dominated by this desire or pursuit. No man will stay committed to a vision without faith, because only a man of faith sees the future as the present. Claiming the promises of God daily keeps a man committed to the task to which he has been called. Hudson Taylor commented, "All of God's giants have been weak men who did great things for God because they reckoned on God being with them." God is not looking for new plans or methods or programs; He is looking for men to carry out His principle of multiplication, resting on His faithfulness and claiming His Word.

David was a committed man. Dozens of times in the Psalms he says, "I will . . . ." Paul enjoined his followers, "Whatsoever ye do, do it heartily, as to the Lord" (Col. 3:23). Our success in reaching future generations is in proportion to our whole-hearted commitment to Christ and to His plan.

Third, there is the law of concentration. Concentrating on the individual while working with the mass is another essential for multiplication. Jesus expounded the concept of the pricelessness of the individual soul. "We're getting statistical paralysis," said C. E. Autrey recently in an address to the Texas Baptist Evangelistic Conference. We must "get away from numbers; keep the accent on saving sinners, not on numbers . . . watch out burning incense at the altar of numbers."[5] Many times we become so number-conscious that we forget the capacity for multiplication of one life that is completely God's.

Nothing subsititutes for personal time spent with one man hungry for God. Without a vision for the individual,

[5] C. E. Autrey, Address to the Texas Baptist Evangelistic Conference, 1960.

no pastor would try to work with one man when the pressure of tradition would make him a pulpiteer. A decision that our ministry will be intensive rather than extensive will change our whole life. Quality begets quantity. It takes vision to disciple a man to reach the mass. If you train one man then you penetrate the multitude. Men with a vision for the individual multiply themselves into others and God gives us bands of discipled soul-winners.

Fourth, there must also be a warm spiritual climate in the local church for the maximum growth of multipliers. New converts need the follow-up care of specially trained church members. When a baby is born, it is immediately taken to a controlled environment, isolated from disease, and only the specially trained attendants care for it. We cannot afford to do less for an eternal soul.

To bring a new Christian into a church where the atmosphere is not strongly evangelistic and of positive spiritual conviction is to impair immediately his chances for multiplication. We must build each new generation of converts into church members who are captivated by Christ. We can begin by separating them as much as possible from contact with listless and cold Christians. Campbell Morgan said, "Lukewarmness is the worst form of blasphemy."

Logically, then, the first contacts of the new Christian with his church, through the Sunday school and other organizations, must be of the warmest spiritual intensity. For this reason the New Member Class, preferably taught by the pastor, and follow-up by the Adoption committee, will ensure exposure to maximum Christianity. Bible lovers are produced by the Spirit where the Word is diligently taught. Soul-winners are most easily trained in a soul-winning atmosphere. The right church environment determines the speed and depth of multiplication.

Lastly, it takes time to build a reproducer. Follow-up is not an act but a process, and it must become an integral part of the total church program. Although a man can be won to Christ in a few minutes, the growth of that man takes weeks and months. When God makes something lasting, He usually takes time. He worked with Abraham for over a generation before that "friend of God" learned the lessons necessary to make him ready for the promised son and heir. Moses spent forty years in the desert unlearning much of his Egyptian background and getting to know God in a new way; it was an eighty-year-old man who led the children of Israel out of bondage. David waited over a decade from the time he was anointed king of Israel before God set him on the throne in Jerusalem.

It took Jesus Himself three years of constant discipling to prepare twelve men for multiplication. Paul was no "ninety-day wonder" either; he spent three years in the Sinai peninsula learning to know Christ. But eleven years later he was acknowledged by the council in Jerusalem as having a special mission to the Gentiles. God never hurries in building men.

To see multiplication really work in a church usually takes from three to five years. But this is not long for the vision to be felt in the total work of the church. A pastor may for a while sacrifice valuable time in working with individuals and when he does not see some progress in a few months may consider the program unproductive. But through multiplication, "a little one *shall* become a thousand, and a small one a strong nation: I the Lord will hasten it in his time" (Isa. 60:22).

As your vision of multiplication grows your church grows with it. Examine the laws of multiplication in relation to your own ministry. By discipling a layman and sticking with him until he wins his first man, you start the chain of multipliers for evangelizing the world and following up your membership.

Questions to Answer

1. What does God promise the man whose life is given to strengthening others? (Isa. 58:12).

2. What were the people of Israel commanded to do in relation to their children? (Deut. 6:2) . Why? (Ps. 78:5, 6) .

3. How far had the gospel been preached in Paul's day? (Col. 1:6, 23) .

4. What two qualifications help a man to be a reproducer? (II Tim. 2:2) .

Questions for Meditation and Application

1. Why won't "addition" reach the world for Christ?

2. To how many "generations" is a man responsible in his follow-up?

3. Where does the chain of multiplication seem to be weakest? Why?

4. Name the five laws which will help you to multiply souls.

5. Have you as yet experienced the blessing of seeing your fourth "generation" for Christ?

6. What do you plan to do to secure soul-winners in your church who will produce reproducers?

PART II
PRACTICAL APPLICATIONS OF FOLLOW-UP

CHAPTER 7

Counseling the Inquirer

Responsibility for follow-up begins when a spiritual decision is recorded.

Billy Graham has said, "The evangelist and pastor are used of the Lord to get the inquirer to third base; it's the counselor that bats him home." But is counseling the new member necessary on a local church level? Unequivocally yes!

Psychologically, physically, and, even more, spiritually, beginnings are extremely important. Early traumatic environmental pressures can damage a child for years. Improper diet in childhood can dull the brain and cripple the body. So, too, a lack of definitive counseling at the beginning of a spiritual decision can dwarf spiritual growth.

Any church would do well to have a Counseling Committee made up of trained personal workers who would individually counsel and encourage those who make decisions Sunday by Sunday. Even when a person has been previously counseled in the home by the pastor, there is an invaluable personal touch associated with lay counseling in the church itself.

Many times neither the church members nor the pastor knows the exact spiritual state of a person coming forward publicly. Some evangelists estimate that up to 40 percent of those making public decisions do not know why they came. In the quietness of a room away from the noise and the eyes of the congregation, the counselor can do business for God, find the person's deepest need, and help him toward a healthy spiritual beginning. Churches are being filled with lost new members and those suffering spiritual damage from previous experiences in churches. Immediate spiritual counseling will prevent many problems and increase the percentage of those who will go on into mature discipleship.

Counseling Environment May Vary

There are a variety of counseling environments being used today in churches. In some churches the pastor or counselors kneel with the inquirer for a brief time during the invitational hymn in view of the congregation. A number of other churches counsel in a nearby Sunday School department or room especially designed for this procedure, taking the inquirers out of the auditorium just as soon as they are introduced to the congregation. The main advantage of this latter procedure is to give the counselor quiet moments to discuss with greater flexibility the decision being made. "Voting" on the member or shaking hands is superseded by meeting the immediate spiritual need.

Procedure for Counseling

After those who have come forward publicly in the service have been introduced to the congregation, all of them should be taken immediately to a counseling area for personal conversation. (To take some people and leave others can cause undue misunderstanding and short-cut the value of counseling both for the inquirer and the counselor.) The Chairman of the Membership Committee should speak to the inquirers who are now seated in a private room, stressing that the church is thankful for their decision and wants to get to know them personally. He may mention his own blessing from the New Member Class and other programs of the church. At the rear of the room, those counselors who have been elected by the church should be standing available to be chosen and matched by sex, age, and general background with the inquirers. This matching can be done easily by an educational worker or someone who knows something about those who have come forward. When the Membership Committee Chairman introduces the counselor to the inquirer, they go into a classroom or selected area where they can feel some privacy.

Qualifications for Counselors

The counselor should be an active Christian with a dependence upon the Holy Spirit and the Word of God. He need not have all the answers, but he must have a listening heart. Sensitiveness to the needs of people will grow as one counsels week by week.

Churches using counseling programs must provide thorough training so that counselors can handle the basic problems of inquirers. The training would include suggestions about the counselor's personal appearance and personal habits of hygiene.

The pastor should ask God for parent-hearted men and women who are willing to share not only doctrine but their lives with those who are new in the church (I Thess. 2:8).

Identifying the Need

A counselor is much like a medical doctor in that he has to make a diagnosis of the spiritual condition of the inquirer by the answers that are given. After an introduction, the counselor should ask a number of questions to discover where the person is spiritually. Some of the following questions have been invaluable: (1) What did you have in mind when you came forward? (2) What decision have you made, or are you making? (3) Have you ever made a decision for Christ before? (4) How in your mind does one become a Christian?

One seventy-year-old lady came by "statement" from another church. As the plan of salvation was presented, she began to cry. When asked if she hadn't already received Christ, she said, "No one ever told me how before." Many people come forward on a transfer of letter basis who have never genuinely been saved. The counselor should give a brief testimony of his conversion, and gently lead the inquirer to share his own experience. If he is hazy in this area, then the counselor should present the gospel to the person as if he had never heard it before.

The counselor needs to find out about the spiritual background of the inquirer. An attractive young lady, the wife of a serviceman, came forward in a large Baptist church that had just started the counseling program. The counselor heard an amazing story. This girl with a Catholic background had married a Baptist boy, joined his church, and been baptized on the statement that she believed that Jesus Christ was the Son of God. No counseling was done. When they moved to another base, at a local church revival she went forward again, feeling a deep need in her life. The evangelist asked her if she believed in Jesus, and she replied, "Of course I do." At another church, after being transferred again, she went forward, prompted by the Spirit, still seeking to fill the void in her life. It was only after all this joining and having all of these abortive experiences that a counselor sat down with her and discovered that she had never understood exactly how one received Christ as Saviour and Lord. After her conversion, she was then scripturally baptized and began to grow.

Meeting the Basic Need

There are five common needs reflected in new-member decisions made on the local church level: (1) the need for conversion; (2) assurance; (3) restoration to fellowship; (4) transfer of letter from another church; or (5) commitment to some area of Christian service.

If the need is clearly salvation, open the Bible, take out a piece of paper where you can draw out either the Bridge of Life Illustration (page 172), the Four Spiritual Laws, or something that will enable you to illustrate the gospel, and then give them a copy of this illustration as they leave. Open the Bible and show them slowly, verse by verse. Ask questions about each verse they read. For example, in Romans 3:23, you might ask, "Who has sinned? What is sin? Does this mean you?", etc.

Ask the inquirer to pray specifically, thanking Jesus for dying for his sins, and asking Jesus to come into his heart now (Rev. 3:20; John 1:12). Get the inquirer to pray aloud, if at all possible, even if you must lead him in this prayer, sentence by sentence. Some of the verses used in the counseling situation can also be used to encourage the person who has just made a decision into real assurance of salvation. After the decision is made, give him the first Gospel of John Bible Study (page 141). Encourage the convert to do this Bible study and tell him that someone will be visiting him this next week to encourage him in his decision. The counselor can then graciously introduce the inquirer to a member of the Membership Committee who will seek briefly to validate the decision indicated on the card.

The Problem of Assurance

The counselor never tells the inquirer that he is saved, under any circumstances. This is the work of the Holy Spirit to use the Word to bring about assurance. People lack assurance of their salvation for two main reasons. Either they have never been saved, or sin has come into the life and has ruptured their relationship with the Lord to such a degree that they have lost the joy of their salvation (Psa. 51:12). The counselor can readily ascertain assurance by asking the person, "If you were to die today, would you go to heaven?" It would be valuable to go over the inquirer's initial decision for Christ, find out when it was made, the circumstances, any pressures that might have caused the decision to be "men pleasing" rather than a surrender of the heart. Let the inquirer talk. The counselor needs insight into whether or not the person is equating salvation with baptism, good works, joining the church, doing what the folks wanted, etc. It is a good procedure to give a gospel presentation to all who lack assurance. At the end of the presentation, simply say, "Would you say that you have as yet experienced Christ in the way that we have been talking about?" If he indicates that he is not sure, then encourage him to pray a prayer of surrender and commitment to Christ now, thanking the Lord that regardless of the past, he is now letting Him in as Saviour.

Many times a lack of assurance is an indication of sin in the life. The counselor should avoid getting the inquirer to unload a garbage can of sins on his ears. The counselor may open the Bible to I John 1:9, and go over the meaning of the words in the verse, stressing "confess"; the counselor should encourage the inquirer to pray silently, confessing all known sin. At the end of his prayer, he may say aloud "amen." Then the counselor should lead in prayer. The inquirer should be helped to a real conviction of assurance that God has forgiven him and forgotten the sin. The "how" of Christian victory should be taught and some specific instructions given to encourage the inquirer in Bible study, a devotional life, the memory of Scripture, and the sharing of his faith.

Problems of Restoration and Rededication

The word "restoration" conveys the idea of encouraging someone back to a previous relationship with God. Restoration means we help the person who has a sin problem. The counselor must lead him to be specific, to confess his sins to God, and to use the doctrine of I John 1:9 as above. The counselor needs gently to probe with questions to make sure the inquirer is aware of God's willingness to forgive and cleanse. The counselor may begin with, "Is there any area in your life where you have not been willing for Christ to be Lord?" Use II Corinthians 5:15, Romans 12:1, and related passages to show the need for Christ to be Lord. The counselor must be Christ-centered in his emphasis. Unless the inquirer becomes vitally concerned about his walk and fellowship with Christ, the counseling will have little permanent effect. The most powerful motivation for a holy walk and Christian service is love for Christ.

Teach the "how" of victory in the Christian life. Talk with him about his prayer habits specifically. When does he pray? When does he read or study the Bible? What kind of daily consistency does he have in these vital areas? Give him a plan to go by. There are suggestions in the Appendix for Bible reading, study, etc. Does he understand how to be "occupied with Christ" (Isa. 26:3)? As one Christian has put it, "You don't get victory. You've got victory. Victory is a Person."

Stress the importance of fellowship with other believers in the church (Heb. 10:25). Isolation from the body of Christ is one of Satan's major tools to keep the Christian from learning and sharing and growing with others. Lone-wolf Christianity is not New Testament Christianity. The counselor may be led to encourage the inquirer to confess the forgiveness which he has experienced to some friend or loved one.

Problems in Transferring Church Membership

The counselor should be unusually enthusiastic and positive in his comments to one coming from another fellowship. There should be an emphasis upon the personal interest of the pastor through the counselor to the needs of the inquirer. The counselor may open the Bible to I John 1:3, explaining that the word "fellowship" involves sharing things together. Then let the counselor share his own personal testimony of salvation and identification with the local church. The inquirer should then be asked such questions as: "How long have you been a true Christian?" or, "When did it all begin with you?" or "What did Jesus do for you on the cross?", smiling and being positive as he talks.

After hearing what he considers a valid testimony, the counselor encourages the inquirer in commitment to Christ and the total program of the church. Many times, however, the inquirer will be unable to give a clear, concise testimony of conversion. While the counselor has been trained that his own personal experience need not be duplicated emotionally in the life of the one being counseled, there must be delicate response to the Spirit of God at this stage. The author's counseling team has been amazed at the number of people who have joined the church as professing Christians and then discover through counseling a need for conversion and who then respond.

Problems of Spiritual Commitment

The counselor has an opportunity to encourage an inquiring heart toward the fullness of God's will. The counselor may stress Romans 12:1, 2, emphasizing that God has a specific plan for every life. Other passages on "why God made us" (Isa. 43:7; Rev. 4:11) give the reason for commitment from God's viewpoint. The counselor should ascertain where the person is in regard to his devotional life, Bible study, Scripture memory, and activities of ministry in the local church; schooling plans and home difficulties should be discussed.

There has been too little emphasis among many evangelicals upon the subject of spiritual gifts. The inquirer should be led to read passages in Ephesians 4, I Corinthians 12, and Romans 12. There should be a guidance in helping the inquirer discover his spiritual gift (I Pet. 4:10). God does not call everyone into a "church-related vocation," although everyone is called to minister in the area of his spiritual gift. The counselor should refer the inquirer to one of the Church Staff so that ministry assignments can be made.

There must be continual encouragement by the church toward those who make commitments involving church-related vocations. Young people should be put on mailing lists for missionaries and denominational youth papers. Young couples should be encouraged by fellowship with the most spiritually alert adults in the church.

Problems Involving Special Needs

People come forward in church services for a variety of reasons. Some come with marital problems, an urgent desire to ask spiritual advice, guilt about something in the past, or because of a burden for a loved one or friend. It is generally appropriate after initial counseling to refer them to a deacon, staff worker, or Sunday School teacher. One of these may be better able over a period of time to encourage an inquirer regularly. The author has found in long-range counseling an unusual response to his recommendation for memorizing verses of Scripture about peace, assurance, forgiveness, and love. Memorization can be a constant tool in the hands of God, changing the mind of the troubled between counseling sessions.

Children present special problems in counseling. They are so different from adults in response, perception, and understanding. The counselor should ask the child questions so that he can let you know exactly what he is thinking spiritually. Watch putting words in the mouth of a child by asking him "yes," or "no" questions. The child will try to please you and say what he thinks you want to hear. Probably the Wordless Book (page 177) is the most practical tool to use along with the Bible in salvation counseling. A child will readily admit to sins, wrong attitudes, and be quite honest with a counselor he feels has had some of the same sins and needs.

After the Counseling

One of the most difficult and important aspects to counseling is the regular check-up to make sure that follow-up is being done in the home of the inquirer. The Membership Committee must have a secretary who will call the person doing follow-up, keep records which show the steps accomplished in the follow-up procedure, and be an encouraging link between the new member, the Membership Committee, and the Pastor. The easiest people to recruit to do counseling and follow-up are those who have had a satisfactory experience being counseled and followed-up by someone else. The program perpetuates itself through spiritual fellowship in the counseling room and at home. Occasionally there will be a counselor whose attitude or ability is suspect in doing an adequate job. Bungling the decision is as bad as damaging the newborn baby. The impressionable new members' needs must take precedence over any feelings of the counselor. The Membership Committee Chairman, Co-Chairman, or Secretary, therefore, must be on their toes to ascertain if any counselor consistently seems to offend or miss the person's basic need. Churches using inquirer counseling regularly have found a consistently positive response. Negative reaction to counseling seems to be less than 1 percent. A church may have only 50 people inquiring a year. Yet, it is important that these 50 have counseling. A counseling program will pay off in changed lives. It is the beginning step in the growing vision a church must have for future generations.

CHAPTER 8

The Adoption Plan for New Members

To "adopt," says Webster, "is to take by choice into some relationship." Each new member in the church should be adopted by an older Christian and helped to grow through a personalized program of Bible study, prayer, and service. Such a procedure is frequently called the "sponsor" or "adoption" plan. Regular church visitation must not be confused with the ministry of a corps of specially instructed visitors. The Adoption Plan is best carried out through a committee of discipled church workers who are the projection of the heart of the pastor, working to develop future lay leadership.

A committee member visits each new member in his home once a week for at least six weeks, seeking to establish contact of a helpful, spiritual nature, to follow up the decision made, and to suggest a course of Bible instruction, devotions, and church-centered enlistment. Through counseling and simple assignments in Bible study (using the Question-Answer Studies in Appendix A, or something similar) and prayer, each new member is guided in his spiritual growth. The lesson plans for home visitation have some of the same content as the New Member class taught by the pastor. The committee member's visitation during the week supplements and personalizes the pastor's teaching on Sunday.

The committee of adoption seeks to visit personally and to teach each new convert, new member, or new family joining the church. Church members who make decisions of consecration also need the encouragement of personal follow-up. New members from elsewhere who are mature soul-winners may be helped for shorter periods of time in the interest of uniformity of teaching within the church. After evangelistic crusades, the need for personal follow-up is great and therefore the Adoption Committee is especially effective at such times.

A Florida businessman with a vision for souls took this idea to heart. With the encouragement of his pastor, he trained over a hundred church members individually or in a class. These one hundred have won and are working with 177 others.[1] Such is the Adoption Plan at work.

Scriptural Basis for Adoption

Moses adopted and discipled Joshua. Through Moses' personal training Joshua was prepared for the responsibility of leading the children of Israel into the promised land. Elijah took Elisha from among the band of men whom he taught in the school of the prophets. Jesus chose the Twelve out of dozens who followed Him in the early days of His ministry. When Paul adopted Timothy, he simply applied the principle of personal training which had been practiced for centuries in developing leadership among the Jews. One man sharing with another what God had taught him became a scriptural blueprint in the structure of the first-century church.

Timothy was in all probability converted at Lystra during Paul's ministry there.[2] As they traveled together, Timothy absorbed Paul's single-visioned purpose and sacrificial love for Christ. Paul commanded Timothy to share what he had learned from him with a faithful man able to teach still others (II Tim. 2:2). This imperative is a practical operating principle for keeping and building each new member in the church.

Multiplied thousands are lost to the church each year because they are left to grow by themselves. If they do not

1 W. B. Moore, "Evangelism in Depth," *The Baptist Standard*, March 1960, p. 7.
2 F. W. Farrar, *Life and Teachings of Paul*, p. 217.

respond to enlistment appeals, they are soon left alone. They need individual Bible study in the home, person-with-person prayer time, and a Christian friend who understands their problems. The pastor may be so busy that it will take weeks before he can make an initial call. In large churches, the pastor may never get to visit all new members in their homes. Through his Adoption Committee, the pastor can, by extension, spend time weekly with the new members.

"Why should we have this special group on top of all the organizations already in the church?" you may ask. The answer is, because this program of building new members is a specialty and needs to be done by specially trained workers. Furthermore, the Adoption Committee gives the new member more personal and immediate help than the New Member class.

Organization of the Adoption Committee

The pastor or an outstanding soul-winner in the church should be the chairman of this committee. Much prayer should be offered by both pastor and church for the right man. If the church has an evangelism committee, its chairman may be considered for this responsibility. He certainly should be a deacon, if at all possible. His job will require much spiritual discernment and maturity. He must be a good visitor himself, and able to devote a considerable amount of time to develop this plan in the church. Also he must know his committee members well enough to match them properly with the new members. Two co-chairmen should be chosen to help him.

Each member of this committee should be either a graduate of the New Member class or a layman discipled by the pastor. After the class is held, those whose hearts are burdened to help others should be voted by the church to represent them on the Adoption Committee. These committee members should be, if possible, soul-winners as well as church boosters. They represent their Lord, their church, and its program to the very impressionable new member.

The committee member must be a pace-setter, faithful in studying the Word, in prayer, and in witnessing. We teach and help others to experience that which blesses our own lives. Only a soul-winner, for instance, can lead the new member into fruitful witnessing. A visitor who is inconsistent in his personal devotions will have little success when trying to urge new members to set apart a "quiet time"!

A Christian who would help others must be open to correction himself. Only those who want to grow spiritually will be able to take admonition. The ability to receive correction graciously and to learn from it is a distinct mark of spiritual maturity.

A useful visitor must be "able to teach others also." (II Tim. 2:2). Some people are faithful in the church but unable to pass on to others what they know. A willingness to share the Word should characterize the members of this committee of adoption. Teachers and officers of the Sunday school, deacons and leaders in Training Union should be encouraged to work in the Adoption Plan. In this way regular church visitation may be synchronized with this most pointed approach to follow-up.

Procedure for Adoption

At the time a person unites with the church on profession of faith, transfer of membership, or otherwise makes a decision for the Lord, the committee chairman should receive two duplicates of the information card, one for himself and one to give to a committee member. The chairman matches the new member with a committee member of like sex, age, and background as nearly as possible. Children can be followed up by mature men or women who are accustomed to working with them. Appropriate Sunday school teachers should be used if at all possible. The matching and the contact between the new member and the Adoption Committee member should take place the *first* week. It will probably be necessary during the initial stage of this program for the committee member to adopt more than one new member.

Following Up the New Member

To assist the committee member in follow-up, a series of "Follow-up Contact Report" sheets have been developed (see end of chapter). They give the visitor a point-by-point summary of material to be covered at each of the six visits with the new member. Each sheet is a *suggested* lesson plan for a visit.

The visitor must always bear in mind, however, that people have widely different needs and problems. No one sheet will meet the needs of all the new members. The visitor must be under the guidance of the Holy Spirit, who promises to guide us into all truth. The Spirit will lead the visitor and make him progressively sensitive to the needs of people in this important work of building lives. The following suggestions give more detailed instructions on follow-up visitation and adoption.

First, make an appointment to visit the person assigned to you during the first week following his decision. Review the notes from the New Member class, and seek to get the perspective of the new member on the material to be presented. Plan the exact material for your first visit, prayerfully reviewing your contact report sheet and your first Gospel of John study. Think through your goal for the visit and the assignments you will suggest for the next week.

Above all, pray daily for the person you are to visit. Pray before you go and keep the attitude of a prayerful servant (Matt. 20:27-28) which is the best foundation for helping the new member. Do not hesitate to refer immediately to your pastor or chairman any problem or question you found difficult to handle during the visit.[3]

3 R. A. Anderson, *The Shepherd—Evangelist,* p. 312.

How to Teach in the Home

1. Try to be alone with the new member if possible. Family groups normally do not lend themselves to an effective teaching situation of this kind. Be diplomatic and flexible, however.

2. Get acquainted with the new member. Be observant of his home and any interesting features about it which will help you to know him better. Notice the books and magazines and any hobby indications. A broad base of common interests will make follow-up easier and more personal.

3. Ask questions about his spiritual background. Explain why you are there, and emphasize the church's desire that he personally grow in practical Christianity. This is accomplished through Bible study, fellowship in the church, daily prayer and witnessing.

4. Use the Bible to answer his questions and problems. Use the time you spend with him to create a relationship based on what God says in the Word. The church you represent preaches and teaches the Bible, and it must be the one standard by which he evaluates life.

5. Be sympathetic and encouraging as you talk with him. Be open to share your personal answers to prayer and to mention difficulties in which God fulfilled His Word for you.

6. In introducing the Bible studies, new doctrines and assignments, tell him why, show him how, get him started, and keep him going. Teach him to share the Word with others, because he will learn to do by doing.

7. At each visit review briefly the lesson from the week before.

8. Adjust the assignments to his individual pace. When he doesn't fulfill his assignments, find out why, but don't drive him; lead him. Perhaps a phone call during the week with an encouraging word will help him get the study done in time for your next visit. Above all, win his friendship and enlist him in the church.

9. Spend twenty minutes to an hour on each visit, as the situation warrants. After the first visit, move quickly into the lesson. Encourage him to talk about it, and ask questions to stimulate his interest. Sometimes a "preview" of next week's lesson will make him want to move forward. Be specific in your assignments and get his promise to have them done when you come for the next visit, for which you make a definite appointment.

10. Keep a notebook in which to record his progress, his problems, the assignments you have given him and your appointments with him.

What to Teach

What we teach on each visit will depend somewhat on whether or not the new member is enlisted in the Sunday school and evening program of the church. If he is enrolled in the New Member class, a program of review and help with its assignments will be most valuable and appreciated.

If he is not yet a part of the church program, consistent follow-up by adoption is most important to bridge the gap between joining the church and enlistment into its total ministry. The Studies in the Gospel of John (pp. 141ff.), together with the contact report lessons, will teach the new member the following:

1. The Gospel, and assurance of salvation (first two Studies).

2. Forgiveness for sin and victory over it. Help him set up a "quiet time" through the prayer list idea in the third John Study.

3. Discipleship through obedience and witnessing. On the basis of the fourth John Study give an opportunity to the new member to give you his testimony and to hear yours.

4. The practical results of believing God. In Lessons 5 and 6 stress the importance of church fellowship and stewardship. Perhaps at this time the financial program of the

church may be presented. Enlistment in the New Member class, in a Sunday-school class, and in the full program of the church comes smoothly and naturally as the result of personal adoption of each new member.

Optional Material

Some new members will simply eat up the studies you bring. Others will move much more slowly. For those whose interest deepens and increases as the weeks go by, special assignments in Scripture memory, visitation, Bible reading and study are available in the Appendices. If the new member desires to meet for longer periods of time after the initial six weeks, the lesson material of the New Member class may be shared.

The pastor or Adoption Plan chairman should go over the next contact report sheets with the visitors at least a week before each is used. He should carefully note the results of the different visits. Some visitors may find it profitable to go out two by two for the first few visits.

Counseling During Invitations

A number of prominent churches have successfully begun to counsel with all who make a public decision during the invitation. The pastor briefly talks with the "enquirer," then introduces him to one of a group of "counselors" near the pulpit, trained through the Adoption Plan. The enquirer is then counseled in a private room off the auditorium, according to his spiritual need. Some churches present those counseled at the next service. Other churches change their order of service so that announcements, a song, and the offering come *after* the invitation. In ten to fifteen minutes all the enquirers, aside from problem cases, are presented to the church. Making this standard procedure will not only develop excellent counselors for evangelistic services but also solve many new-member problems.

FOLLOW-UP CONTACT REPORT — *First Week*

1. Pray before you go to visit your contact, making sure that there is no known sin in your life. Ask the Spirit to make you usable; then expect God to work through His Word.

2. Get acquainted with the contact. Be friendly, positive, and open. Get him alone if possible, and let God guide.

3. Pray with him. Audibly praise God for his decision and ask the Lord to make your time together profitable and enjoyable. Encourage him to pray aloud, also.

4. Go over the first "Gospel of John Study" with him. If it has not been given to him already, hand him one and explain it carefully. If he already has it, go over it with him. Tell him *why* the study will help him in his Christian life. If you give him the study yourself, help him to get started by going over it with him, showing him how to look up the references and how to write the answers in his own words. Leave Lesson 2 with him, for him to do during the week before your next visit; suggest that he do at least three questions every day. Get his promise to work on the study regularly and to have it ready next week.

5. If you see that he is hazy on the Gospel or uncertain in his assurance of salvation, draw the "Bridge of Life Illustration" for him.

6. Proceed slowly; keep everything simple. You are dealing with a babe in Christ, or probably someone who has never attempted this sort of thing before. Talk "with him" not "down to him"; keep your language simple and non-technical. Repeat again and again until he grasps what you are teaching. Question him to be sure that he understands your presentation. Show him how Scripture relates to his daily life.

7. Make an appointment that is convenient for both of you for your next meeting. Think through ahead of time what your own schedule is and how many times you can

meet with him. The same time and place helps to build a habitual natural contact situation.

8. Check on his plans for Sunday school and church attendance the next Sunday. If he is not yet enrolled in the New Member class stress its importance both to himself and his church. Encourage him to go, and offer to take him if needed. Close your session together with prayer.

9. *Optional*: Leave either a Gospel of John or some other help which will assist him in daily Bible reading. Suggest that he read at least 15 verses every day, preferably in John's Gospel. (See Appendix A for other reading helps.)

10. Return this sheet to the committee chairman or pastor with your signature and answers to the questions listed below.

I MET WITH ....

on .... at .... p.m.

YOUR NAME ....

CHECK UP (encircle fitting word)

1. Contact was (enthusiastic, warm, cool, negative) at the visit.

2. Grasp of material covered seemed (good, fair, poor, very slow).

3. Person did (not) have assurance of salvation when I left.

4. Person has (not) promised to be in Sunday school this coming Sunday.

5. I have (not) volunteered to bring him to church.

FOLLOW-UP CONTACT REPORT — *Second Week*

1. Pray before you visit. Ask the Lord to cleanse you and prepare you for your assignment. Pray for the contact's interest.

2. Greet your contact enthusiastically. Before you pray together, ask him to share any need or request.

3. Review last week's lesson briefly. Be specific; ask questions. Does he remember the content? Encourage with sincere praise and love. You are building on last week's foundation: the contact should know what it means to be a Christian, to have assurance of salvation, to know the gospel and to remember the "Bridge Illustration."

4. Go over Lesson 2 with him. He should have it filled out; if not, *ask him why,* and wait for the answer. Perhaps you did not really convince him of the value of the study. Remember the five steps to follow in teaching: tell him why, show him how, get him going, check up, and teach him to reproduce. Always stress the practical application in these John studies. The doctrinal content is basic for equipping the new believer against the attacks of Satan. Ask him questions on his assurance such as, "If you were to die now, what would happen to you?" Assurance is needed for growth.

5. Be patient and plain in your teaching. Depend on the Holy Spirit to speak to his heart as you teach the Word. Be willing to go slowly again and again over a truth.

6. Leave with him Lesson 3 and get his positive committal to do it. Encourage him by finding his spiritual interest and showing him how these lessons will help him toward this interest. He must be led in love to see that consistent time with God each day is essential if he is to grow and amount to something spiritually.

7. Start him on memory work with I John 5:11-12, a verse on assurance to meet Satan's attacks of doubt. Stress the value of having God's Word in the heart. Share your own joy in Scripture memory. *Optional:* Give him the "Beginning with Christ" pack,[4] asking him to read the instructions and memorize the first verse.

8. *Optional*: Check up to see how he is coming in his daily reading of the Scriptures. Never give an assignment of any

4 Printed by The Navigators, Colorado Springs, Colorado. Priced at 10c each.

kind without checking up — make this an accepted part of your work with your contact.

9. Return this sheet to the committee chairman or pastor with your signature and answers to the questions listed below.

I MET WITH ....

on .... at .... p.m.

YOUR NAME.........................

CHECK UP: (encircle fitting word)

1. Contact was (enthusiastic, warm, cool, negative) at the visit.

2. Grasp of subject covered last visit was (good, fair, poor).

3. Response to material covered this visit was (good, fair, poor).

4. Contact has problems (no problems) with his decision thus far.

FOLLOW-UP CONTACT REPORT — *Third Week*

1. Pray before you visit. Last week's blessings and challenges are not enough for today. Receive fresh power from God.

2. Meet your contact warmly and heartily. Pray with him.

3. Review last week's lesson: Always *review*. Have the contact recite the main content of what you covered together. Check him on his memory verse. If you gave the "Optional" pack, check him on introductory content and the verse. Assign I Cor. 10:13 or more verses from the pack, according to his interest and pace.

4. Show him possible personal applications from Lesson 3. Stress in this lesson the believer's walk in victory through the Word, and his privilege of prayer.

5. Discuss the prayer list idea. Help him set up a prayer list and emphasize the value of specific prayer. His list should include the members of his family, his unsaved friends, job associates, his church, pastor, denominational interests, and missionaries. Suggest a minimum of fifteen minutes each day for his "quiet time."

6. Share with him your own experiences of victory through daily prayer.

7. If he is coming along nicely in reading the Word, memorizing and doing the John lessons, then give him Lesson 4 for the next visit. If he is slow, help him get caught up and reassign what he has failed to do.

8. *Optional*: Suggest he write out his testimony for sharing it with you next week. It should involve three parts: his life before accepting Christ, how he came to be saved, and what his life has meant since he became a Christian. It should be written out in non-theological language so that the unsaved can understand it. Encourage him to complete this assignment.

9. Be flexible; give assignments to match his spiritual growth and pace. Adjust each visit to meet his specific needs, rather than to complete the work in a specific time. There is no *definite procedure* in meeting the needs of others. Seek the guidance of the Spirit in suggesting assignments for him. Make a definite appointment to meet with him again next week.

I MET WITH ....

on .... at .... p.m.

YOUR NAME..........................

(Put comments or suggestions on back of page)

Is your contact enlisted in some phase of the church program? If so, what?

Where lies his chief interest?...........................

....

FOLLOW-UP CONTACT REPORT — *Fourth Week*

Aside from those you are "building as babes" in Christ, you should have among your church friends a man or woman whom you are "adopting" to give spiritual help, usually a believer who has had very little personal discipling. Why not make an appointment and take him to visit the contact with you this week? He can visit along with you and observe. Perhaps in seeing the new member's growth, he will be encouraged to apply for membership in the Adoption Committee, or perhaps be convicted of his need for more personalized study in the Word. Use your own judgment as to taking a friend along.

1. Have prayer with your friend in the car before going to make the visit.

2. Introduce your friend to the new member and briefly explain his presence. All of you have a short word of prayer at the beginning.

3. Have your contact give a résumé of main points of last week's lesson. Check him on his assignments. Did he have victory in his "quiet time" this past week? Does he know his memory verse? Does it mean anything personally to him? How is he doing in daily Bible reading? Does he like the prayer list idea? Any answers to prayer?

4. Go over Lesson 4, or whatever assignment you suggested to him. If he wrote out a testimony, share your own testimony and ask him to read his. Offer helpful suggestions. How is he progressing in church?

5. *Optional,* according to time and progress: "Bridge of Life Illustration." Show him how he may share it with someone else. Help him "select" some unsaved friend to whom he may witness and give the illustration this next week. If the contact himself is slow in grasping the illustration, ask him to hand out a Lesson I with a Gospel of John instead. If the contact is enthusiastic, ask him to give a Lesson I to the person to whom he shows the "Bridge

Illustration." Answer any question on witnessing he may have. Ask him to let you know when he feels he can witness to someone else so you can pray for him.

6. Give him Lesson 5, and assign I John 1:9 for him to memorize. Go over the verse with him, if time permits. Explain the need for immediate confession of all known sin. Ask him to be able to explain the "Bridge Illustration" next week.

7. Make a definite appointment for next week. Try to set up a visit to witness to an unsaved person for your next time together.

I MET WITH ....

on .... at .... p.m.

I brought ....along with me on the visit.

YOUR NAME.........................

Is there anyone specific your contact will witness to this week?...................

Who is it? ....

Are you going to accompany him? ....

FOLLOW-UP CONTACT REPORT — *Fifth Week*

Within the past four visits you have learned much about your contact, and a relationship has been established, a bond of fellowship has been strengthened for the church. Your goal in any contact with others is to help him grow in the knowledge and love of his Saviour. If your contact is progressing, you may want to spend time with him or his family other than just the Bible study time each week. Perhaps you might plan for your two families to get together socially. Or the two of you might go to a street meeting, visitation, or other activity together. Notice especially how your contact is fitting into the program of the church. Is his family also enlisted?

1. Have prayer with your contact. You should be growing

more and more sensitive to his deepest needs and spiritual weaknesses.

2. Teach or review the "Bridge of Life Illustration." Draw it for him; he need not know the references from memory now, but should take notes and mark references in his Bible. Did he give out a Lesson 1 and a Gospel of John? Have him quote his memory verse, I John 1:9.

3. Emphasize the need for his sharing Christ with others. He has completed his witnessing Bible study and now needs to apply it. Encourage him to write out his testimony, and give it. Help him find some definite evangelistic outreach at work, at home, or in his neighborhood. Offer to go with him. Get him praying for at least three unsaved friends or relatives. If you are a witness, he will "catch" the spirit of boldness which God has given you. Go out to witness *that* night if possible; use the "Bridge Illustration" as the Spirit leads.

4. If you remain in the contact's home, go over Lesson 5. Teach him how to "claim" a promise. Help him choose at least one verse in the study which he will claim in believing prayer. A verse should always be claimed in regard to a specific need, person, or desire. Have him put this verse and the request together on his prayer list.

5. Assign him John 16:24. If he has been good in memory, you may increase the number of verses you assign each week to two or three. The "Going On With Christ" pack is available for this. If the contact has been unable to complete work previously assigned, do not give him Lesson 6 for the next visit. Plan to go over work already assigned, and make an appointment for your next meeting together.

6. If during visitation together a soul was won to Christ, make plans to visit the new believer together during the following week. Emphasize to your contact his responsibility to help the new believer grow and get into the church. Suggest what he might do to help the new believer.

I MET WITH ....

on .... at .... p.m.
                 YOUR NAME ....

We (have, have not) visited an unsaved contact together.
Results: ....
....
....
....

FOLLOW-UP CONTACT REPORT — *Sixth Week*

In this last *scheduled* meeting with your contact you should make whatever plans possible to help the person go on for Christ. If it is possible to meet with him further and he is progressing satisfactorily, then you may desire to share with him truths which you have found useful from either the Personal Evangelism or New Member classes. Visitation evangelism should be continued as God leads. Opportunities to witness should be presented to your contact through every avenue of the church program. If the contact is cool and indifferent, then you may consider this meeting as final. But you should continue to remember him in prayer, asking God to get across through some other medium these basic truths so vital to growth and maturity.

1. Pray with the contact. Ask about his answers to prayer. Help him to enlarge his prayer horizon by remembering together church missionaries and foreign countries in need of Christ.

2. Discuss the opportunity to do visitation evangelism which you had last week. What were the advantages gained? Was the presentation of the gospel clear? Did the contact give either a clear testimony of salvation or present the "Bridge Illusration" satisfactorily? Both of you should learn from the witnessing together.

3. Go over Lesson 6. See how well he was able to "break down" a verse by meditation. Give him the fruits of your

own meditation on John 16:24. Make sure he has the basic rules for meditation.

4. Check him on his memory verses. Share the blessings of consistent memory with him. Give your own testimony of the power of "hiding the Word in the heart" (Ps. 119:11). Help him get started on further memory work by suggesting these verses: Psa. 119:9, 11; Matt. 6:33; Phil. 4:13. Or if you like, hand him the "Going on With Christ" pack and suggest he start with the first two verses for next week.

5. If he as yet does not have a consistent plan of Bible study, study the following questions to answer after either daily Bible reading or chapter reading: in the passage is there (1) a promise to claim; (2) a command to obey; (3) a blessing to thank God for; (4) a sin to forsake; (5) a prayer to use as his own; (6) an example to follow; (7) the best verse; (8) the main lesson; (9) something to learn about the Godhead? Have him keep a notebook for *writing* down what he learns day by day.

6. Leave him on a positive and encouraging note of challenge and love. Express your heart concern and willingness to meet with him again, if he desires. Set up an appointment if possible, centered in Bible study, prayer, and witnessing. Encourage him in faithfulness in the church, taking sermon notes, etc.

I MET WITH ....

on .... at .... p.m.

YOUR NAME ....

Please give a *short* summary of the six weeks time spent with this contact, your impressions, his needs, etc., on the back of this sheet.

CHAPTER 9

Church Integrated Follow-Up

"Evangelism is not evangelism at all unless it wins the whole life," says W. E. Grindstaff.[1] And according to A. C. Archibald, "A study of statistics from all major denominations for the past twenty years reveals that nearly forty per cent of our evangelistic recruits are lost to the church within seven years."[2] The church should give to the newly won convert a balanced program of growth; the goal of soul-winning is a life captured for Christ.

Every organization in the church should be an avenue for building the believer or its place in the church is useless. Many churches have isolated the responsibility for following up new members to only a few segments of the total church program. That this plan has not succeeded is attested by church rolls with thousands of names whose bearers are unseen, unknown, and unused for Christ.

Scriptural evangelism and follow-up are God's means for keeping, developing, and multiplying the church membership. "The true test of evangelism," declares R. A. Anderson, "is not how many come into the church to worship, but how many go out from the church to serve."[3] Lives on fire for Christ are the only statistics we dare offer to God. Through church-integrated follow-up, we begin to deal realistically with unchurched, unenlisted, unfruitful, and nonmultiplying believers.

Gaps in Church Follow-Up

There are four problem or gap areas in the church through

1 W. S. Grindstaff, *Ways To Win*, p. 201.
2 A. C. Archibald, *Establishing the Convert*, p. 13.
3 R. A. Anderson, *The Shepherd—Evangelist*, p. 297.

which believers are lost or their spiritual growth is interrupted. Follow-up through personal contact will bridge these gaps in our churches.

There is a gap between winning a person to Christ and getting him into the fellowship of the church. Normally, what do we do after a soul is won? Is it not the usual practice to invite him to join our particular church? But then, if he is reluctant because of childhood training or division of family membership, we eventually leave him alone.

Would it not be wiser for us to give follow-up care anyway? The convert could be visited by an Adoption Committee member, counseled on his problems, given assurance of his salvation, and trained in Bible study and prayer. Through care on the part of a church member, the new convert can be loved into a willingness to join the local fellowship. Church membership then becomes the fruit of initial follow-up, and this gap is closed.

The second gap is between joining the church and being enlisted in its program. The majority of those attending services have little to do with the building up of the church; a few must carry the burden of the many. Generations without follow-up care have left the church full of Christians still needing to apply the basics of Bible study, prayer, and witnessing. "Unless we can in some way establish habits of private prayer in the lives of the thousands who unite with our churches, we shall, at best, only partially conserve them," is the opinion of Archibald.[4]

The problem of enlistment is difficult. To some extent, this gap will be closed as the flow of new members is directed into the Sunday school, the New Member class, and the Adoption Plan. The backlog of unenlisted members will eventually have to be reached through personal visitation; in the home the real reason for their unenlisted state may

4 *Op. cit.,* p. 48.

be discovered and resolved.[5] The visitor could do a simple Bible study such as one from the "Gospel of John Series" with them. Many members will respond to such ministry to their needs with a renewed zeal for Christ. If you would increase what a man does for Christ, you must of necessity deepen his personal relationship with Christ.

But enlisted members are not necessarily soul-winners. This is the third gap area. Members wrongly depend on church services to give the major evangelistic thrust of the church. "We do not need more preaching nearly so much as we need people who will apply the spirituality generated in our services of worship to the task of persuading friends to accept Christ and His program of living," says Kernaban. "Our public services of worship should be for inspiration, education, and culture of our people. Our evangelism should be done just as Jesus did it—by personal contact and interview."[6]

As the pastor takes a deacon or Sunday-school teacher with him in visitation evangelism and continues to teach the Personal Evangelism class, some of the enlisted leadership will be led into a strong soul-winning ministry. On a church-wide basis, the "Bridge of Life Illustration" (pp. 172ff.) can be taught to the adults and perhaps the "Wordless Book" (pp. 177ff.) to the children so that every member may have at least one way to present the gospel. The gain in the number of *new* soul-winners each year is a true standard of the church's follow-up progress.

Winning souls is no substitute for producing reproducers, however. This is the fourth gap area in church follow-up. Soul-winners can only be multiplied as each is trained to teach those he wins to witness to others. The soul-winner learns this multiplication emphasis from the pastor, an Adop-

[5] Ask the INACTIVE: "When did you come to know the LORD; tell me about it. Are you satisfied with your Christian experience up to now? In your opinion how does a Christian grow? Has anyone ever helped you to grow, through personal Bible study in your home?"

[6] A. E. Kernaban, *Visitation Evangelism*, p. 118.

tion Committee member, or the Personal Evangelism class. If you disciple a soul-winner, he will soon disciple the one he wins to be a soul-winner.

Advance Preparation for Follow-Up

The local church must assume total responsibility for all those reached through its members during the year. "Responsibility of the church for nurturing of converts grows out of the fact that they have voluntarily committed their lives to the church for development ... They believe in the church and upon entering it are enthusiastic and idealistic. They look to the church as their foster mother."[7] We must therefore make definite "arrival plans" for those converted during regular visitation or evangelistic meetings. Members of the Billy Graham team begin to prepare for counseling and follow-up as much as six months in advance of a campaign. Let us focus on the advance preparation needed for church-integrated follow-up of new members.

The pastor must plan into his church calendar the teaching and evangelistic ministries essential to integrating follow-up into the church. Foundational to the church's follow-up program is the pastor's personal ministry with one or two consecrated laymen. In a lesser degree couples also can be trained in small groups to take responsibility in various phases of church follow-up which the pastor himself initiates. In the first year, the New Member and Personal Evangelism classes are begun and the Adoption Committee organized to follow up new members and develop soul-winning and soul-building personnel. The optimum time for beginning such a program would be six to eight months before an evangelistic crusade.

In the Appendices you will find samples of some effective literature which may be mimeographed ahead of time. Other suggested literature for follow-up should be ordered from publishers well in advance of the need.

[7] Archibald, *op. cit.*, p. 20.

Effective literature, used as a tool, will help to make follow-up easy and practical. It is, however, not the answer to the problems of the new believer, and a top-heavy emphasis on literature will drown your convert under pages of print. The Word of God did not become printer's ink, but Flesh and Blood. Correct follow-up is to present Christ and His answer to life's problems through the Bible. Rely on literature and you will fail in follow-up; rely on Spirit-taught men and women with a heart for discipling others and literature becomes a useful tool.

Initial Follow-Up

Follow-up logically begins at the time a person responds to an invitation. Those who take information from the new member print the pertinent data clearly on card forms and at least three carbon copies should be made. After the service, one card goes to either the pastor or the educational director, one to the superintendent of the Sunday school, and two copies to the chairman of the Adoption Committee. When a committee member is assigned to work with the new member, he receives one card, while the chairman keeps the other copy for future check-up.

"Magnify the reception of a new member," advises C. E. Autrey.[8] Recite to him before the whole church some of his responsibilities and opportunities as he becomes rooted in the fellowship, asking the members of his family who are present to stand with him. Always encourage the church members to extend personal greetings of welcome to each new member after the services.

When a family joins the church, it is a nice gesture to present them with a copy of the Bible autographed by the pastor. A personal written word of encouragement inside the cover will help to make this Bible a treasured part of the home. Invitations to special social gatherings should always be given to all the new members. Especially after an evan-

---

[8] C. E. Autrey, *Basic Evangelism*, p. 146.

gelistic campaign a dinner to honor the new members and converts, at which they are the guests of the church, will help to get them into church fellowship more quickly.

Before the new members leave the building, the pastor should secure an appointment with them and the first Bible study lesson in the Gospel of John (p. 141) should be explained to them by the Adoption Committee chairman. Included with it should be a mimeographed sheet labeled "Important Notice," to inform them that the pastor's representative will visit them during the week to introduce the Adoption Plan and help them in Bible study and church orientation. The notice must also state that a special class, required for all new members (the New Member class) will begin at a certain date. It should be explained to them what it is, when it meets, and how they can profit from it. Thus the new members are prepared for further church contact.

Giving an interest questionnaire along with other literature on the policy and program of the church aids in finding the best use for the new members' experience or talents. Churches desiring information more quickly about new members that come from other churches can send a confidential questionnaire to their former pastor which he can remit with their church letter.

Secondary Follow-Up

The pastoral appointment should be a time for discovering any personal needs in the new member's life and fortifying him with scriptural answers. At this meeting he is enrolled in the Sunday school and Training Union and encouraged in the stewardship program. A list of practical books for the Christian may be suggested to him (p. 136). When an appointment cannot be arranged, the pastor should send a form or personal letter to each new member emphasizing his joy in their coming, encouraging them to do the Bible study lesson in the Gospel of John, and offering personal help or spiritual counseling at any time.

Information on the new member from all sources is given

immediately to appropriate department or organizational leaders for enlistment. The new member should be given some kind of responsibility in the church program very soon. "Use them or lose them." *Belonging* is a part of the blessing of church membership; but there must be outreach also, if spiritual balance is to be maintained, because we learn to do by doing. In finding a place of service for the new member we must remember, however, the scriptural command not to give a new believer or novice any responsibilities out of character with his new life in Christ. Getting the new convert into some of the training classes or study courses is excellent preparation for mature service in the church.

The Adoption Committee member should visit the new member during the first week after his decision. The procedure outlined in the chapter on the Adoption Plan should then be followed.

Give new members an immediate outlet for witnessing for Christ. A time of testimony as part of regular services gives opportunity for them to express what their salvation or new church membership means to them. Some churches do not baptize a convert until he has enough understanding of his salvation to give a brief testimony in the baptistry. This sort of service is one of the best means of outreach evangelism toward the convert's unsaved family or friends. Some pastors use a short testimony by the convert which has been taped ahead of the service to play when he is baptized.

As the follow-up program is established in a church, those who have top-leadership posts must assume responsibility for the teachers and workers in their departments. The leaders can keep informed on the spiritual progress of their teachers by means of the teachers' and officers' meetings.

"Every church officer, Sunday school teacher, in fact every worker in any department of the church should have under his care a person, preferably a new member, whom he is training to take his place," advises S. W. Powell, writing on conservation.[9] In the same way, the teachers must "adopt" their pupils and guide them in their devotional life and witnessing.

This emphasis in personal follow-up and soul-winning must begin with the church staff to reach the total membership. Experience in soul-winning and follow-up should be an important criterion for selecting a part-time or full-time church worker. In this way all the progress of the church — music, education, teaching, and social events — eventually results in souls being won and trained personally by the members.

What To Do Now

1. Closet yourself with the Lord in prayer and make sure there is nothing in your own life to hinder follow-up in your church. We reproduce what we *are,* not what we would like to be.

2. Never miss observing your daily "quiet time," apart from sermon preparation and study.

3. Begin to pray specifically for a missionary vision on the part of your denomination that includes every country around the world. Ask God to send laborers from your own church to meet the needs.

4. Set specific standards and goals for progress in your personal life regarding your time with the Lord, your witnessing, your mastery of the Bible.

5. Set goals for your church's progress in evangelizing the area of its influence. Make plans for systematic gospel witnessing to every person in your community and city.

6. Move slowly in getting this program under way in your church. Many will not understand the need and you will have to lead them gently in love as you walk ahead a step at a time.

[9] S. W. Powell, *Where Are the Converts?* p. 111.

7. Beginning *now*, ask God for a faithful man. Start with one, or at the most two, and meet personally with them weekly. You begin multiplying your ministry the moment you have trained a man to do what you would do in a given situation.

8. Share your life, your vision, your work, and your heart with other men. Start taking a man with you as you do visitation evangelism. Train him to win his first man and follow that one up until he in turn wins his first man. Work always with others in the context of a training situation.

9. Share your vision and plans with other pastors, one by one. Pray for your denomination's state program of evangelism and follow-up. Lead your church to be an example of follow-up and producing reproducers.

CHAPTER 10

The New Member Class

Anyone who has made a decision for Christ should be carefully and quickly followed up with instruction in Christian living. Lessons in the New Member class explain those few basic doctrines and principles which every church member should know and practice to grow consistently in Christ. Practical needs of the young or immature Christian are met by teaching and discussion of such topics as salvation, assurance, Christ our life, forgiveness, Bible study, prayer, and witnessing (Appendix C).

To build strong discipleship on a weak doctrinal foundation is impossible; it is unwise to take knowledge of the Bible and a spiritual background of any new church member for granted. Unless the new member is already a consistent soul-winner and soul-builder, it is best to start him out much like others who are new believers. The supplementary Unit I in Appendix C has been found especially useful in encouraging new church members to take this vital New Member class instruction.

Putting new members into the same class with new converts for instruction does not imply that their former pastor did not properly instruct them; it merely affirms that consistent instruction is necessary to build a church where every member has basic Christian principles firmly fixed in his consciousness and is committed to the application of Bible doctrine to his own life.

Goals of the Class

To make instruction a required part of church membership is to demand very little; early church history records that classes of instruction were given in the church to all who wanted the privilege of fellowship with a local group of believers. A new Christian should not have to wait months to hear a sermon on how to pray or how to do Bible study. Such immediate needs will be met quickly through the New Member class. What is good material for the average Sunday-school class is not necessarily the best diet for the new believer any more than a normal adult diet is suitable for infants. The New Member class gives the spiritual infant enough preparation to profit from the sermons, Sunday school, and Training Union in the regular program of the church. The goal of the New Member class is the permanent, consistent development of the spiritual life of every believer by establishing right spiritual habits early in his spiritual infancy or church membership.

Sometimes dozens, even hundreds of people come forward each year during the services to express their need for victory, or to confess sin, or to ask for prayer, or to surrender themselves to Christ. To allow these to slip out of the channels of effective service through lack of sealing the decision with scriptural knowledge is a great waste. We may shake hands in church and get them working more than ever; but without instruction on the "how" of forgiveness, victory, and the life of faith, their decisions will probably need to be renewed in a matter of weeks. Every decision must be immediately pegged down with practical Bible teaching applied to the daily Christian walk. This means either extended personal counseling or specific class instruction in the basic principles of Christian living, some of which perhaps they have not known. The church member may be more readily attracted if this class is called "The New Life" or "Discipleship Class."

Preferably the pastor should teach this class. If that is not possible, either the educational director or a gifted Bible teacher and soul-winner should do it. Class instruction, however, is never a substitute for individual contact; it is limited by differences in age, sex, background, temperament, and mental ability of the students. A Spirit-led teacher, sensitive to these differences, can be mightily used by God in this effort.

Many who decide for Christ are children. They should have their *own* class, taught by an experienced Junior or Primary teacher. The same subject matter may be covered, adapted to their age and Bible background. Visual-aid board, illustrations such as the Wordless Book (pp. 177f.), and other attractive teaching tools will be helpful. Those enrolled in the regular New Member class should not be younger than thirteen years of age.

Time is vital in the conservation of the fruit of evangelism. Some follow-up should begin within twenty-four hours after a person's decision. The new believer is an entirely different person from the enlisted, well-indoctrinated Christian. He is a baby, with the same characteristics of a physical baby: helplessness and dependence.

What should we teach, then, and how? Certain time-honored doctrines have long been shared with the new Christians. These usually have to do with the church, its government, and the ordinances of Baptism and the Lord's Supper. These things are scriptural and are a needed part of any teaching program. However, they are not enough. Teaching must proceed from meeting the immediate needs of the new Christians to more advanced instruction.

"First things first" is always true in teaching the new believer. Therefore, we emphasize the order of the class subjects to be taught. While a few church doctrines may be taught in two to four class periods, it is rarely possible to ground a believer in the essentials of Christian living in only a few weeks; the class should extend, if possible, for at least three months. The progression in the subject material is that used most widely by those who have specialized in the follow-up of new believers.

Of course, every believer is different, and there is no one method that is invariably successful. Selecting instruction material is much like mixing a formula for a new baby: the doctor adapts it to that baby's special needs to secure the best balanced diet for maximum health and growth. So also the teacher, through patient prayer, guidance, and practice, must emphasize those doctrines which reach the maximum number of pupils. Asking, and encouraging them to ask, questions can do much to keep the subject matter tailored to the needs of his pupils.

The subject matter of the New Member class parallels the main doctrines taught in the Adoption Plan contact report sheets. (Chap. 8). This is done deliberately so that committee members can later review this New Member material and adapt it individually to new church members and those who were not able to take the class.

Suggestions for the Class

1. *Time.* The class should be held when the most new members and new Christians can attend. However, most pastors use the Sunday evening hour during the Training Union before the regular church service. Start a regular class roll, using the record system of your department normally used at this time. Unless the opening assembly program is brief, it is better to keep the class together for the entire hour. The New Member class will help to establish regular habits of attendance and encourage participation in the church program after finishing the course.

What to do with those who join the church during this twelve-week period? While it is difficult to teach a changing group, each new member should be brought into the class when he joins the church and remain in it until the twelve-lesson series has been taught. By using the Adoption Plan, every new member is being worked with personally, whether he attends the New Member Class or not.

2. *Teacher.* Giving the new student the best instruction is the way to get him interested and keep him enlisted. It gives the pastor his great opportunity to build potential church leadership according to his standards. The relation-

ship between the under-shepherd and the new lambs in his flock is deepened and broadened through this weekly contact, and he is in a position to deal with any potential problem which may arise in their lives. The small amount of time invested thus produces rich returns. By teaching the first few quarters himself, the pastor will be able to train at least one teacher thoroughly equipped to take over this specialized work.

3. *Facilities.* An informal grouping around a table or in a circle is recommended for a small class. This encourages questions and prevents the idea that this is just another "preaching service." Make good use of a blackboard. Some of the illustrations included in this book (Appendices A and B) were designed for the purpose of teaching Bible doctrines and principles of the Christian life, and have been used over the years with marked success.

Make sure the members bring a Bible with them every time. The central foundation for teaching is what the Bible has to say. By continually answering their questions from the Bible you will develop their trust and confidence in God's Word, an attitude which every believer must have to be a consistent witness for Christ.

Ask the class members to take notes — most of them will find it a reasonable request. It is a good preparation for doing the same thing during the church service where you certainly want them to take notes. A good notebook $3\frac{1}{2}''$ by $6''$, or larger, should be used for listing the subjects and suggested assignments given in class. Taking notes increases interest in the subject, stimulates thinking, and prevents the church member from brushing off the sermon before he gets out the front door. What a man does not remember cannot help him spiritually. Emphasize the fact that God requires of class members to remember His Word just as much as He requires of the teacher or preacher to prepare the Word for their hearts. It is good to go over Hebrews 2:1 in this connection: "Therefore we ought to give the more earnest heed to the things which we have heard, lest at any time we should let them slip."

4. *Instruction.* Use non-technical, simple language in teaching the class. If you want them to learn the definitions of certain doctrinal words, explain the words before you use them continuously. Ask questions frequently and have a period for asking questions by the students each session. Also ask for testimonies of how the Lord is helping them and speaking to them during the week. Ask them to tell others about the grace of God during the closing time of prayer and sharing. Something they recently received from the Lord does more to encourage others to seek God for themselves than anything else. Remember, telling alone is not teaching, and listening is not necessarily learning. If they cannot live out what they learn, and pass it on, the time and effort you have shared with them is unprofitable and they are deceived (Jas. 1:22).

Encourage every person to pray a sentence prayer in the class before the group is dismissed. As confidence builds and knowledge of the Scriptures increases, then the length of time given to prayer may be proportionately increased.

5. *Assignments.* Make assignments clearly and carefully. Let them know that what you suggest they do is for their own growth and blessing. Always remember the basic pattern for teaching: tell them *why*, show them *how*, get them *started*, and always *check up* to see how they are doing. Inquire privately why an assignment was not done and spend time personally with those who fail to do their assignments for two successive weeks. We must be "gentle unto all men"; for their own sakes, however, we must require production according to their spiritual ability. To let a man go week after week without completing the assignments not only damages him spiritually, but also wrecks the class spirit for doing the job together.

6. *Discipline.* Discipline is a distinctly spiritual matter and can definitely affect a Christian's total life and fruitfulness

in Christ. There is no well-trained soldier without discipline, and discipline in building disciples is essential. Verses such as Ecclesiastes 8:11 and II Timothy 2:24, 25 are for the teacher; and Ecclesiastes 9:10; 10:10, Jeremiah 12:5, and Colossians 3:23-24 are good verses for the student.

One of the finest young men I have known, now overseas as a missionary, was a "coaster" in his church until he was exhorted by a small fellow whose life was disciplined for Christ. The young man had never before been talked to so forcefully about his walk in Christ. First, he was surprised, then angry, then amazed, then convicted. The incident opened up his heart for further instruction, and his life was conserved for full-time service for Christ. It takes more Christian love and courage to point a man to his needs than it does to pat him on the back and approve his mediocrity.

7. *Order.* A suggested order for class teaching is: Opening prayer, review, lesson, assignments, question time, sharing, and closing sentence prayers. Since each teacher will want to teach his own church's particular doctrinal and organizational emphases, the lessons in Appendix C are supplementary. These seven lessons stress "the Christian's Relationship and Responsibility to Christ." If this series of lessons is given to the new members first, they become a good foundation for stressing the particular church's doctrinal and spiritual emphases. All church teachers and officers should be encouraged to take the New Member class to standardize the teaching in the Sunday school and as a background of information for the Adoption Committee members. The pastor may desire to teach this material on prayer meeting night or at another time during the week just to these key church leaders. Those who do the assignments will make the best workers in the church follow-up program.

The Personal Evangelism Class

A yearly Personal Evangelism class is recommended to develop soul-winners and soul-builders in the church, conserve the faithful and interested graduates of the New Member class, and strengthen the outreach of the church toward the lost. Many pastors have already developed such a class; but for those who have not, the following nine-week period of emphasis is suggested.

In the first two weeks, emphasize the personal life of the soul-winner — his devotional life, his commitment, his understanding of the Christian life. Witnessing is the overflow of life in Christ, and we must be in daily fellowship with Him to "bear much fruit."

Throughout the nine-week course, make assignments in Bible study, Scripture memory, meditation, and application of the Bible to life. Begin memory assignments with verses from the Bridge Illustration, so that these illustrations may be used early in visitation.

During the witnessing classes (4 weeks), teach the soul-winner to present the Bridge Illustration to adults, and the Wordless Book to children, and give assignments to carry out during the week. Have him write out his testimony (pp. 189f.), and make him practice giving it to others. Discuss the reasons why people do not witness and the problems encountered in witnessing. Send the class out in visitation evangelism two by two.

Devote the remaining three weeks to follow-up. You might introduce the four ways to follow-up, its scriptural basis, and how it can be done in your church by teaching Chapter 3 and parts of Chapters 2, 5 and 8 from this book. Give out the first Adoption Plan report sheets during the first of these three classes (Chapter 8), so a new member can be assigned and visited by the soul-builder during the sessions of the remaining two classes. Problems encountered in "Adoption" visitation can thus be referred to the teacher. Some members of the Personal Evangelism class may want to continue work in the Adoption Plan.

The Personal Evangelism class may be taught by the pastor or a soul-winning layman. The procedure for each class

is: check-up and review, presentation of new material, and
outside assignments in the field. An occasional quick test
on the assignments, with presentation of case studies and
questions as to what Scripture verses to give a person will
enliven the presentation. The class could be taught at an
early hour on church visitation night since it will be developing visitors adept at soul-winning and follow-up. A good time
for beginning the Personal Evangelism class is three months
before a scheduled evangelistic meeting; in this way a group
of personal soul-winners can be prepared for this meeting
and a number of individuals readied for follow-up of the
evangelistic results.

CHAPTER 11

The Home Bible Class

Every believer's home is his mission post in his community. It is surrounded by people who need the Saviour. Each Christian home represents an extension of the church to that neighborhood.

To a group of first-century believers at Philippi, the Holy Spirit gave the command that they should "shine as lights in the world, holding forth the Word of life" (Phil. 2:15,16). For almost three hundred years the early churches used private homes as basic meeting places for united prayer, teaching, and fellowship. The Scriptures record the growth of the church through these home meetings.

Unfortunately, in the minds of many modern Christians only the "church on the corner" is identified with all that is true evangelism and Bible teaching, and some have opposed any meeting outside the church building. The fact is, however, that lay leaders trained by the pastor can direct home Bible studies adequately and they have proved to be for the growth of the church. We have to admit that much of the amazing success of cults and splinter groups in securing thousands of proselytes is to be attributed to their house-to-house teaching.

Remembering the New Testament use of the home, we may again utilize it effectively as an extension of the church in the community. The Christian home can be not only an evangelistic mission station, but also a member-building agency and a training center for teachers. Unsaved people who are interested in knowing what the Bible has to say usually feel more comfortable, less on the defensive side, and more open to teaching in a home than in an unfamiliar church environment.

The home class can become the initial step toward a number of mission churches through your church. Thus the goal of a home Bible class is either evangelism or follow-up through simple Bible study. For evangelism, the class may center around community contacts and friends. Among Christians of the same denomination, the goal is follow-up through systematic Bible study. In this way, both new and old members will be strengthened in a Bible-centered environment *during* the week. Bible teachers and leaders for home classes may be elected by the church and will be under the personal direction of their pastor.

Lecture Method of Bible Study

The lecture method of Bible study is the one used most frequently for growth and fellowship in home Bible classes. The instruction centers around a Bible teacher who does most of the studying and speaking. The lecture-type study can put the student in contact with a great amount of knowledge in a short period of time. However, telling isn't teaching and listening isn't necessarily learning. Bible study differs from normal Bible reading in that the student writes something down which he has found in his reading; the extra thought process in writing helps the student remember what he has read. In a Bible class, assignments help the new student to apply vital knowledge to his life experiences.

One drawback of the lecture method is the danger of the class becoming teacher-centered. When he or she is sick or out of town, the class may stand still and the students not move ahead in personal growth. This type of study does not seem to develop teachers rapidly because there is usually less class participation. But even with its limitations, this method of study does supply the student with basic information and can give systematic teaching and encouragement through an experienced teacher.

"Self-feeding" Method of Bible Study

The "self-feeding" or discussion Bible class encourages consistent study habits in the student. When each class member is responsible for doing some part of the preparation, everyone is in a position to take part in a general discussion. The discussion group is made up of people interested enough in personal Bible study to work on a lesson *beforehand* and write it out. Assignments should fit the general ability of the class, and regular check-up at each class period will help stimulate members to a higher standard of work.

Although someone must lead the group discussion, he acts as a guide rather than a lecturer. As a class grows, the leader must always be seeking to develop others capable of leading the group. By requiring participation and weekly preparation, he encourages the students to establish study habits that help them become good teachers.

When the pastor trains these group-study leaders, there is no need for him to attend the classes. A layman-led study not only challenges the students to dig for themselves but makes it easier to bring in unchurched contacts. The unsaved, as a rule, should not be invited to this kind of study. It is very difficut to set standards of work for the unsaved because they do not have the hunger and discernment of the believers. If someone is bringing an unsaved contact, the group should be alerted to his status.

Some "self-feeding" groups may plan one meeting a month especially for unsaved contacts. To such a special meeting each member of the group may bring an unsaved neighbor or friend. An experienced soul-winner should be in charge and passages that stress the Gospel should be studied, using the question-and-discussion approach. One or two planned personal testimonies add to the effectiveness of the gospel presentation.

The Evangelistic Study

The evangelistic study takes the message of Christ to the community and the homes in need of salvation. This study may be a combination of the lecture and "self-feeding" types. The home in which the group meets may be either that of a church member or an unsaved contact. The evangelistic study should, as a rule, be free of hymn singing and everything that smacks of a church service. The study leader should plan on one or two short personal testimonies in keeping with the backgrounds of the unsaved visitors. Bibles are provided for all who attend.

The leader should summarize the Scripture passage after it is read aloud by individuals in the group, and his leading questions help underline the doctrines pertaining to salvation. Always use the Bible to answer questions asked by the unsaved. The Person of Christ revealed in the Word must be the center of any evangelistic study. Some excellent study passages are the Gospel of John, chapters 1, 3, 5, 19 and 20. Some suggestions for study booklets to use are found toward the end of this chapter and in the Appendix.

Churches using evangelistic studies in homes report splendid results in souls won, new members acquired, and better-trained leadership. One church in Dallas has some 150 Bible study classes meeting weekly all over the area.[1] The sponsoring church's membership has increased substantially and strong penetration has been made into unreached neighborhoods. They have fulfilled Christ's command to go with the Gospel where the people are.

Preparation for a Successful Class

Four weeks prior to the first class the pastor should select the leader and two assistants. A week later a meeting with the leader and assistants should be called where materials for study are distributed and definite plans made for their proper use in the class. A home should be prayerfully selected from the church membership, and two weeks before the class meets personal letters must be mailed to prospective students or interested unsaved contacts in the immediate community. The pastor gives the prospect list to the leader and his assistants and any notes on individual needs of prospec-

[1] David Enlow, in *Moody Monthly*, Oct. 1959, p. 20.

tive students are made at this time. A time of prayer and sharing is suggested for the pastor and his study leaders in their last planning meeting for this follow-up or evangelistic penetration.

A mature layman soul-winner should lead the class. He need not be a Bible scholar, but must be someone who will feel responsible to prepare himself well through study and prayer. He must be able to stick to the point and not be sidetracked. No leader should be selected who has not been in close contact with the pastor or educational director for personal discipling. Thus the pastor is in constant contact with the study leaders and can get accurate reports on the progress of the group.

Two assistants should be chosen to follow their leader, and are to stimulate the discussion with comments and questions as needed. Another of their functions is to help the leader to seek out and meet the needs of individuals in the class during the informal coffee time at the close of the meeting. Difficult problems are referred to the leader or pastor.

The leader and his assistants must have mastered all the study materials used for class work. A successful study group will encourage the formation of other groups. Mission churches may eventually be organized from a number of expanding study groups in one area.

When there are at least two individuals or couples who are interested, a weekly home Bible study may be organized. A convenient night should be cleared on the church calendar for this study time. An hour and a half is a maximum meeting time.

The size of the class should be limited to twenty members. Invitations by letter and visitation should be made to potential class members either by the leader or by his assistants. First, warm personal notes should be sent to the prospects announcing the meetings, their purpose, and the time, and that the recipients will be contacted a little later. A letter from the pastor to new members can encourage them to attend the Bible study in their area. Follow the letter up with a short personal visit and offer transportation if needed. Make sure that the prospect can easily find the home where the study is to be held, and be sure to leave its phone number with them.

In selecting a home, certain requirements must be considered. It must be well lighted and easy to locate; and the room where the meeting is to be held should be large enough to accommodate the class comfortably. It is nice to have a piano, although this is not necessary. Many married couples will be able to come only if they can bring their children. For this reason there should be some place in the home where children can play apart from the meeting area. A mature woman should be recruited to supervise the children to relieve the hostess of this responsibility. The children who are old enough to listen may be taught Bible stories while younger babies are put to bed.

Students should come with Bibles or New Testaments, paper and pencil, and, above all, a willingness to learn. Have extra Bibles ready for those who may forget their own. After each class a report should be made to the pastor on the attendance, future prospects, and counseling problems.

Suggested Agenda for First Class

1. Give out attendance slips to class members as they arrive; pin name cards on everyone.
2. Start on time with a welcome and introduction by the leader. If the group is small, have each student introduce himself. A word of testimony is permitted here, depending on the type of class.
3. Summary of material to be covered in the class by the teacher or leader.
4. Prayer by leader or assistant.
5. *Optional:* singing led by an assistant, and/or two three-minute testimonies on salvation for the evangelistic study.

6. Bible instruction-discussion period by leader (thirty minutes).

7. Further discussions and questions from students. A time of practical application of the lesson to life should be a part of every class.

8. Assignment and materials for next class by teacher.

9. Prayer by assistant.

10. Close exactly on time, one hour from beginning of meeting.

11. Fellowship time with coffee. All students are free to go. This time is excellent for making contacts with students.

Agenda for Subsequent Classes

1. Start on time. Pass out attendance slips and name cards.

2. Greetings to newcomers by assistant.

3. Prayer by assistant.

4. *Optional:* singing led by assistant, or testimonies.

5. Brief review of the last class by teacher or leader.

6. Check for completed assignments around the group.

7. Instruction or discussion study period by leader and students.

8. Question-answer period; stress application of lesson.

9. New assignment and handing out of appropriate materials.

10. Prayer by assistant.

11. Close on time, one hour from start of class.

12. Fellowship and coffee time.

Suggestions for Class Leaders

1. Begin prayerfully, expecting God to work and use His Word in people's lives.

2. Start the class on time and dismiss on time.

3. Have good eye contact with your students; be friendly and personable.

4. A sense of humor helps keep the group with you.

5. When teaching, ask questions around the class. Prepare thought-provoking questions ahead of time; come prepared with Bible answers.

6. Stick to the lesson — stay out of trouble. Relate all questions to the lesson only.

7. Be careful not to "point a finger" at your students. Include yourself whenever possible in statements of exhortation.

8. Let your Bible-study content and discussion be Christ-centered.

9. Lead and teach so that the class will go away "seeing Jesus"; stay away from building the class on yourself.

10. If the subject of denominations is introduced by the students, give Bible answers to their questions. Seek by personal contact after the study to encourage students to attend special services of your church from time to time. Be especially careful about bringing up your own denomination in a "mixed group."

11. Know your lesson; there is no excuse for misdirection and thoughtless preparation by the leader. Have a daily "quiet time."

12. Meet with your assistants regularly; go over the contents of each lesson with them; teach them how to emphasize doctrine with leading questions.

To aid the leader and the assistants in formulating questions, the following points are suggested:

1. The questions should have a definite answer in the Scriptures.

2. They should stimulate thought and be interesting.

3. They should call out a main point and add to the strength of the Bible verse; they should be essential.

4. They should be suited to the mental and spiritual capacity of the group.

After the lesson, a time of fellowship is suggested. This will be an informal social gathering with coffee served by the hostess. Its purpose is to secure closer contact between the leader and assistants and those needing spiritual help. Every student should be met personally, and any special needs noted. In deference to the host and hostess of the home, the leader is responsible to see that everyone departs on time. Further discussion may continue outside, or through appointments made for later in the week. The hostess has the option of serving more than coffee, but put no unnecessary burden on her. Expenses may be shared, but not by students in an evangelistic class.

Materials for Bible Study

In home studies where students come from many denominational backgrounds, mimeographed materials are best. To use "denominational literature" as such can impede the study and force issues that need not be raised. If you wish to use appropriate denominational study literature, mimeograph it. The subject material is chosen according to the needs and spiritual age of the students. Salvation, the Word, prayer, obedience, and witnessing should be the underlying emphases of most new classes. Teachers who use the lecture method may expound a book of the Bible. Most groups, however, will not have a gifted teacher and hence special study booklets for the new Bible students need to be introduced.

For the beginner in Bible study some Question-Answer studies are printed in the Appendix, pages 138-158 These were written especially as introductory studies to use with the unsaved, new Christians, and in home study groups. Start the class out with single-sheet studies, preferably the Gospel of John Series; after having used from four to six studies, move to other studies included in this section.

Other evangelical Bible study booklets available are: (1) *The Alpha-Omega Series* (especially Philippians).[2] (2) *Introductory Bible Study; Lessons on Assurance; Lessons on Christian Living* (with memory work attached) ; *Christian Character Course.*[3] (3) Through the Bible Study (question-answer study on each chapter of the Bible).[4]

The individual pastor should examine any booklets used in his church program of Bible study to choose those best suited to the group. Other methods for more advanced Bible study are listed in Appendix A. Each leader should seek to develop future teachers from the group, to teach in the Sunday school and to organize other study groups.

The Children's Bible Class

Since children comprise the dominant group to accept Christ in our churches each year, it is reasonable to expect that children's Bible classes can be a prime source of neighborhood conversions. An aggressive children's program in the church will bring multitudes of unreached children and their parents to the Lord. "Considering that today two-thirds or twenty-eight million American school-age children are not attending *any* church or Sunday school, it is all the more important that Christians awaken to the challenge of the Bible club for children in their homes," says David Enlow.[5]

As in the vacation Bible school, the goal is the building of young lives for a lifetime of service for Christ. In the home Bible study, the gospel of Christ's love is presented to children. They thrill to the stories of Joshua, David, Paul, etc. The most responsive ages for this group are five to thirteen. A graded system of classes may be instituted when the teacher has a large mixed age group and several assistants.

By teaching a children's Bible class, a mother can have an

[2] Alpha-Omega Series (Nashville: Convention Press).
[3] The Navigators (Colorado Springs, Colo., Box 1861).
[4] Through the Bible Series (Dallas: Through the Bible Publishers).
[5] *Op. cit.*

evangelistic teaching ministry without the necessity for a baby-sitter or automobile. Mothers with children in grade school are particularly good teachers for this ministry. By taking responsibility for a home class, mothers will find a new world of service for their Lord.

The teacher must not only be someone who loves children, but she must also be willing to spend time to win the children and their parents to Christ. Although an inexperienced person can easily learn children's Bible stories, it takes time and prayerful study to become sensitive to the work of the Spirit in young hearts.

Each teacher should have at least one assistant, usually the mother of some of the children who attend the class. The assistant recruits and gathers up the youngsters, keeps them orderly, helps prepare refreshments, and generally acts as a dependable extra arm of the teacher. She need not be a Christian; dozens of assistants are won each year through hearing the Gospel taught in such classes. Many assistants become so interested in this ministry that they start children's Bible classes themselves.

Organizing the Class

As you visit and invite the children, you may help their parents become co-operative by leaving an open invitation for them to attend the class at any time. While you are not interested in parents attending the classes regularly, an invitation does give them confidence in you. Your willingness for them to attend discourages any doubts they may have, any fear that you are trying to "steal" their children for your church.

Have the class weekly after school for one hour in a home that is conveniently located near where the children are: if possible near a grade school or in a neighborhood with many children. A typical meeting will include songs, stories, and refreshments. Having contests to get the most new members and visitors will build attendance. As children are saved and begin to grow as Christians, their new life provides opportunity for experienced church visitors to contact whole families.

Suggested Agenda for Children's Bible Class

1. Welcome children enthusiastically; introduce new ones.
2. Have opening prayer (after a few weeks you may be able to call on members of the class to pray for their church, the missionaries, their friends, etc.).
3. Sing two or three songs (motion choruses, gospel songs, and hymns the children know; to sing the liveliest songs first is a good rule).
4. Teach the Scripture memory verse for the week.
5. Review last week's lesson; ask questions about it.
6. Lesson: a Bible story (fifteen to twenty-five minutes).
7. Application of lesson to life; invitation with gospel presentation for the unsaved children.
8. Sentence prayers or testimonies; announcements about next week's story.
9. Closing prayer by teacher.
10. Light refreshments.

Materials for Teaching Children

The longest period of the study hour is given to teaching through the use of object lessons, pictures, and flannelgraph illustrations. These teaching mediums provide a focus of attention and help increase the children's interest. The flannelgraph is one of the best tools available to get truth across, but there is a danger that interest in the picture itself may become greater than the truths you are trying to illustrate. Any visual aid is simply for the purpose of illustrating the doctrine being taught.

The quality and quantity of good flannelgraph materials are increasing. The series put out by the Child Evangelism Fellowship (Grand Rapids, Michigan) are very practical and inexpensive, and each series of twelve lessons on a topic provides thorough doctrinal coverage. They are: "The Life of Christ," "How to Pray," "The Bible, the Word of God," and various Bible stories. Scripture Press (Wheaton, Illinois) also offers colorful one-lesson stories in flannelgraph.

The "Wordless Book" has been an effective instrument in presenting the gospel for over fifty years (pp. 178-182). This little five-color booklet forms the basis for telling the plan of salvation in a simple way that children can understand. One lay evangelist uses it with adults, too, and hundreds are saved each year in his services. It has been found useful with both children and adults in evangelistic crusades, and also for teaching Christians to witness. Although the Child Evan-gelism Fellowship is not the originator of the Wordless Book, they print them as a service; the price of a booklet with instructions is ten cents. Every teacher in the church should be familiar enough with the Wordless Book to use it often. Also, children love making their own booklets.

One evening the author brought to a prayer meeting a seven-year-old who had recently accepted Christ at a home Bible study in another part of the city. The child gave his testimony in the church service, using the Wordless Book. Adults were amazed that a child so very young could be taught to present the plan of salvation, and many came after the service asking to be taught how to use the booklet to teach their own children. With such a tool, children can be taught to witness to their friends and bring them to Christ.

That master-preacher of the nineteenth century, Charles H. Spurgeon, once said that a child five years of age, properly taught, was able to receive Christ and live the Christian life. D. L. Moody frequently used the age of six in referring to salvation awareness in children. Christ Himself said that childlike faith is necessary to enter the Kingdom. It should be understood that these classes are not to compete with any church program for the saved child. Through this program of home Bible classes, adults and children yet unreached and unenlisted can become saved and trained for service.

MEDITATE
Psa. 1:2; Josh. 1:8; I Tim. 4:15

MEMORIZE
Psa. 119:11; Deut. 6:6;
Deut. 11:18; Prov. 7:1-3

STUDY
Acts 17:11; II Tim. 2:15

READ
Rev. 1:3; I Tim. 4:13

HEAR
Rom. 10:17; Rev. 2:7, 17,
29; 3:6, 13, 22

PART III

APPENDIX A

HOW TO STUDY THE BIBLE

The *hand* is an excellent illustration to demonstrate how the Word of God may be appropriated into the life of the Christian.[1] There are several ways of fulfilling God's command to "let the Word dwell in you richly in all wisdom."

The fingers of the hand represent "avenues" by which the Word of God may be appropriated. Let us look at each finger to see its function in getting the Word into our life.

The *little finger* can be said to represent our capacity to "hear" the Word of God. "So then faith cometh by hearing, and hearing by the Word of God" (Rom. 10:17). We hear the Word of God as it is preached in church, discussed in Sunday school and by conversations in fellowship with other Christians. Try holding your Bible with your little finger. Impossible! But by coupling hearing with meditation (the thumb) you get a little grasp on the Word. It is very easy to pull it out of your grasp, however, isn't it? Thus it is when you only "hear" the truths of the Bible. They are soon lost to you.

The *ring finger* represents appropriating the Word of God by "reading." Paul said to Timothy, "Till I come, give attendance to reading" (I Tim. 4:13). In Deuteronomy 17:19 a king was admonished to "read therein all the days of his life: that he may learn to fear the Lord his God, to keep all the words of this law and these statutes, to do them." In like manner, as we read our Bible faithfully, and meditate, or think on its truths, we grow in appropriating it to our lives. Now, if we hold the Bible between our thumb and our little and ring fingers, we have a better grip. Yet it doesn't take

---

1 Hand diagram used by permission of The Navigators.

too much to remove it from our grasp. So also reading and hearing alone will not give us a solid grasp of the Word of God for our lives.

The *middle finger* can be thought to represent "study" of the Bible. "Study to show thyself approved unto God" (II Tim. 2:15). By systematic, prayerful study of God's Word the basic truths of the Christian faith are imparted to us. The Bible says, of itself, "All scripture is given by inspiration of God, and is profitable for doctrine, for reproof, for correction, for instruction in righteousness: that the man of God may be perfect, throughly furnished unto all good works" (II Tim. 3:16,17). Thus by studying, reading, and hearing the Word of God, along with meditation, we obtain a good grasp of the truths for our daily walk with the Lord. Yet we can have a still better grip on the Word.

The *index finger,* the trigger finger, represents one of the quickest and most effective ways to gain a working knowledge of the Bible. Through memorization we are enabled to "write it upon the   table of the heart." Memory gives us ready access to God's Word to aid us in witnessing and to help us have victory over sin. In Psalm 119:9 we read, "Wherewithal shall a young man cleanse his way? by taking heed thereto according to thy word." The Psalmist speaks to the Lord saying, "Thy word have I hid in mine heart, that I might not sin against thee" (v. 11). So we are challenged to hide the Word of God in our hearts — to memorize it.

Now our illustration takes on real meaning. With all the fingers working together with the thumb, a firm grasp may be had on the Bible. The *thumb* is used to represent "meditation" on God's Word. In Joshua 1:8 we are commanded to ponder on the Scriptures, "This book of law shall not depart out of thy mouth; but thou shalt meditate therein day and night, that thou mayest observe to do according to all that is written therein: for then thou shalt make thy way prosperous, and then thou shalt have good success." Note also the promise of Psalm 1:2-3.

By hearing, reading, studying, and memorizing, coupled with meditating on the Word of God, we make it available for application in our lives. Not one way, but all five are commanded and commended to us by God. Only as we get into the Word and get His Word into us can we live a consistent, victorious Christian life.

How to Use the Hand Illustration in the Church

Hearing the Word (pp. 134f.): We forget 90 percent of what we hear: note-taking in the church services will double the percentage of our take-home response. Contests with Juniors and emphasis on note-taking through adult classes can increase each member's application of the Word.

Reading the Word (p. 135): We forget 60-80 percent of what we read. Emphasis on the eight suggestions will deepen Daily Bible Reading results in the life. Also with something definite to find, spiritual truths will become more evident for application.

Studying the Word (pp. 158ff.): The Study the Scripture study will help Sunday-school teachers in lesson preparation, develop future teachers as students begin to do personal study weekly, and will give pastors a plan of chapter analysis which can be shared with laymen. Other types of study, especially the Question-Answer studies (pp. 138-158) will be the initial doorway for building a Bible study program in the individual life.

Memorizing the Word (pp. 163ff.): For the amount of time invested, Scripture memory is the finest help toward a balanced life of usefulness in the church, from witnessing to teaching and speaking. Other church members will find mutual stimulation through the growth of those who memorize Scripture.

Meditating on the Word: Coupled with each of the above, meditation creates opportunities for the Holy Spirit to make Bible truth and Christian doctrines practical and useful in the daily life of each believer. The meditation suggestions (pp. 165f.) are useful with daily Bible readings, for preparing devotionals, and for any serious study of a single passage or verse.

Each section of the Appendix will be readily useful in some way, either in individual lives or in the total church program, depending on the needs of the local church. The pastor should prayerfully examine the materials, print them, and use them most carefully.

Hearing the Word

Speaker ....

Subject ....

Scripture Text .... Date ....

Message Outline or Exposition Points:

1. ....
....

2. ....
....

3. ....
....

Other Verses Used:

1. .... 4. ....
2. .... 5. ....
3. .... 6. ....

Application to My Life:

1. The main idea ....
....

2. The most important Scripture verse to me.............
....

3. What did God say especially to me through the message?
....
....

4. Is there anything which God would have me to do?...

....

5. Whom can I help by telling them some truth from this message? ....

....

....

PURPOSEFUL BIBLE READING

Many Christians have become disinterested in reading their Bibles, and consequently given it up altogether. One reason is that they can't seem to recall what has been read, or to relate it to life. They "explore" the Bible. The "purposeful" reader looks for specific things. He is going somewhere and will come up with something valuable in his reading.

The goal of Bible reading should not be to gain information alone, but to change our life. While the Bible will inspire and challenge, God desires to conform the reader unto the image of His Son through prayerful meditation and obedience. As you read a passage or a chapter, ask yourself if you can find:

1. A command to obey.

2. A promise to claim and believe (any conditions?).

3. A sin to forsake or an error to avoid.

4. A prayer to echo, or something for which to praise God.

5. Something about God the Father, the Holy Spirit, or Jesus.

6. The best verse.

7. The main lesson.

8. Something from the above which you can apply to your life now.

Keep a devotional notebook. Record promises on a promise page. After you find some of these things in your passage, prayerfully choose at least *one* and relate to your life. Suggestion: Use this list as a guide with your daily Bible readings during "quiet time."

SUGGESTIONS FOR STARTING A LAYMAN'S HOME LIBRARY

AIDS TO BIBLE STUDY:

1. *Young's Analytical Concordance* or *Crudens Concordance* (much smaller). Find any word anywhere in the Bible.

2. *The Treasury of Scripture Knowledge* — 500,000 cross references verse by verse through the Bible.

3. *The New Testament* (Williams' Translation) or *The Amplified New Testament*.

4. *A Topical Text Book* — arranges the Bible by subjects for easy reference, either with whole references or a few words.

5. *Halley's Bible Handbook* — handy factual reference book on the whole Bible.

6. *The New Bible Commentary* by Davidson — an excellent one-volume commentary.

DEVOTIQNAL-MEDITATION BOOKS:

1. *Abide in Christ,* by Andrew Murray (31 daily devotions; a classic).

2. *My Utmost for His Highest,* by Oswald Chambers (daily devotions for every day in the year).

3. *The Christian's Secret of a Happy Life,* by Hannah Whitall Smith (practical classic).

4. *Life on the Highest Plane,* by Ruth Paxson (devotional-life commentary).

EVANGELISM-MISSIONS BOOKS:

1. *Every-Member Evangelism,* by J. E. Conant.

2. *The Life of Hudson Taylor* (2 vol.), by Mrs. Howard Taylor, or *Hudson Taylor's Spiritual Secret* (condensation, abridgement).

3. *Goforth of China,* by Mrs. R. Goforth.

4. *C. T. Studd, Athlete and Pioneer,* by Norman Grubb.

5. *Bill Wallace of China,* by Jesse Fletcher.

Methods of Bible Study

Through the years many different methods of Bible study have been produced and proved helpful in the lives of millions of Christians. Bible study differs from Bible reading in one important point: writing thoughts down. In study there is one more thought process involved, that of writing. Most people interested in the Bible have had very little instruction in this tremendous difference, and therefore are missing the blessings of Bible study and its potential for spiritual growth.

There are five characteristics of a good Bible study we would mention. Although many studies used by pastors and Bible teachers reflect some of these points, only those studies that combine all five are ideally suited for training laymen in study.

It is original. The main characteristic of a good Bible study is original investigation. Reading lessons or materials on the Bible, such as reference books or commentaries, is not original study. The student should come fresh and openhearted to a passage of Scripture. It is the Holy Spirit, the Great Teacher, who should have first chance to reveal the "hidden treasures" of God's Word. Reference books should be consulted after prayerful meditation and diligence fail to bring light to a passage.

It is systematic. For successful and profitable study, we must have a goal before us and be able to finish with a feeling of accomplishment. "If you don't know where you're going, almost any road will get you there." This quotation is indicative of how most people study the Bible — they do a bit here and a bit there, without system, plan, or purpose. Be specific!

It is written. There must be some way to record the thoughts God gives to us so that we keep them applied in our lives and can share them with others. Without writing down ideas and making notes, much time is wasted because we have nothing permanent we can keep. It is so easy to forget the work of God in our lives. "Writing it down" helps us to grow in Christ.

It is communicable. Only what we can share with another is really ours and a part of our lives. A study must therefore be simple enough for the average person to learn. Many Bible studies are not communicable. They are a great blessing to a few people in the church, but are too complicated for the majority. The pastor can't easily pass on his Greek or Hebrew studies. He needs a method of study which he may share with his congregation, teaching them so that they, too, may enjoy the Word on their own and share it with others.

It is personal. The Bible has been given to us to change our lives, not just to enlarge our heads. Bible facts without Bible application will produce only deadness: "the letter killeth, but the Spirit maketh alive." We must learn to see the Scriptures as God's orders and directions for our personal life.

These are the five basics which should be a yardstick to measure any study we seek to use with laymen.

God has given the Bible for the blessing of everyone, not just the minister. The following Bible studies have been found valuable and useful for all ages in varying degrees. Helpful books on Bible study are listed in the Bibliography.

QUESTION-ANSWER BIBLE STUDY LESSONS

The Gospel of John Series

The series is an excellent introduction to the whole field of personal Bible study. It incorporates the five major characteristics of a good Bible study: original, systematic, involving written reproduction, communicable, moving toward personal application. This simple group of topical studies (pp. 141ff.) is of great value in many different and varied situations. Think through the possible use of these studies in relation to your church, to the new converts, and to the unsaved.

For the Christian:

1. Use these studies in the New Member class, where new members become acquainted with your church and its Bible-centered ministry.

2. Use these studies in the Personal Evangelism class to introduce Bible study to its members and thus provide them the first material for passing on what you give them to their unsaved contacts.

3. The series may be used along with other tracts or booklets given to the new member. The church will find them valuable as minimum Bible-knowledge requirements for church membership. Our church requires all new members to complete these studies at the rate of one a week for the first six weeks. Making such studies a church requirement not only adds to the foundational knowledge of the new member, but through the years will raise the standards of the whole membership.

4. Some pastors go over these studies with the whole church in prayer meeting, taking a lesson a week. Begin to incorporate these studies into the church program by using them with any group of youngsters thirteen years of age and up as an introduction to future Bible study, both individual and group.

5. The Junior-graded Lessons 1 and 2 (pp. 152ff.) may be used with juniors and some primaries, followed by Lessons 3 and 4 from the adult series.

6. Use these studies as a weekly basis for the Home Bible Study groups of the church. Because they are inexpensive to produce, they may be used freely, one a week, when starting new groups in which the same people do not appear every week.

For The Unsaved:

1. Include Lesson 1 (with church address printed on it) with all Gospels of John handed out in street meetings, door-to-door witnessing, and other occasions.

2. If your church has any radio or TV broadcasts, offer free home Bible studies to all who write in to the church for them. One nation-wide radio program (UNSHACKLED, sponsored by the Pacific Garden Mission in Chicago) has been printing and offering these studies to their listeners for over five years. Many souls have been saved, many Christians strengthened, and many lives blessed through this ministry of the Word coupled with radio drama.

3. On your church "visitor cards" provide a place where your guest may indicate his desire to have one of the studies. And as such people are visited later, the John study makes an excellent opening for presenting the gospel to the unsaved, for rekindling a cold-hearted Christian, or for emphasizing your church's stress on personal Bible study to prospective church members.

4. Use Lesson 1 for visitation evangelism, giving it out to people who want to witness to a neighbor but can't get started somehow. All sorts of "brush contact" with people give opportunity for starting them off or following them up with these lessons. (It is well to remember in mimeographing or printing these studies that your orders should decrease gradually from Lesson 1 down to Lesson 6. Print about twice as many of No. 1 as any other lesson; the same amount of Nos. 2 and 3; then less, but the same amounts of Nos. 4-6. Remember, in planning your printing, that you will give a Lesson 1 along with Lesson 4 to the students in the New Member class to start their witnessing. Line space so that you print each lesson on only *one* page) .

Volunteers from the Adoption Committee should grade the completed studies. It is also suggested that a card be kept for each member who does the Bible study. When Lesson 1 is completed and returned, make out a card (preferably one on which you can quickly and easily check the study completed, and the date, along with the name and address of the student) .

Be sure to grade these lessons generously at first so that

you will not discourage students. (Suggested grading: A: all correct; A—: one question missed; B: two questions missed; B—: three questions missed; C: four questions missed; C—: five questions missed. But no lower grade! If the lesson is that incomplete, someone should work with the student personally.

PERSONAL BIBLE INVESTIGATION COURSE
GOSPEL OF JOHN SERIES

Lesson 1 — New Life

This course will help you discover facts from God's Word which you need to live life at its fullest. Through this study you will gain an insight into the mind of God, increase your knowledge of His will, and learn more of His plan for your life.

To answer the following questions, just look up the Bible reference from the Gospel of John, think through what the verse means, then either complete the blank *in your own words* or circle the letter which you think is the most correct answer. Pray for guidance. Use only the references given to answer the question. Let God teach you the Bible.

1. Why *was* the Gospel of John written? (20:31 — John, chapter 20, verse 31) . ...
   ....

2. What is eternal life? (17:3) a. Getting baptized. b. Living by the Golden Rule. c. Knowing God and Jesus personally.

3. Why do only a very few people live a genuine Christian life? (5:40) a. They are sinners. b. They won't come to Jesus. c. They don't understand.

4. Where do we find the truth about Jesus? (5:38-39).
   a. In newspapers and religious books. b. By believing what people say. c. In the Bible.

5. People without Christ in their hearts prefer evil to good. Why? (3:19-20). a. Because they can't help it.

b. Because there is greater pleasure in evil. c. Because they choose not to come to the light of Jesus and be saved.

We have found that the Scriptures give us the truth about Jesus, that all men are sinful and in rebellion against God and His perfect will and plan for their lives so that they will not come to the "light of the world," His Son Jesus Christ. Now we shall see God's judgment on sin, and His revelation of His great love for us that we may *live!*

6. Who is able to take away our sins? (1:29,36) ......

7. What happens to those who do not *let* Jesus, God's lamb, take away sin? (8:24; 3:36) ....
   ....

8. At the trial, what fault was found in Jesus? (18:38; 19:4) ....
   ....

9. Why did God let His only Son die on the cross? (3:16)
   ....
   ....

10. After His death, how was Jesus buried? (19:40-42) ...
    ....
    ....

11. What happened to Jesus after He had been in the grave three days? (20:9, 12, 17, 20) ....
    ....
    ......;..

12. What word means the same as "believe" in 1:12?...

13. Have you ever received Jesus into your heart as Saviour and Lord?..............If so, when?.............
    ....

If you are a child of God you have personally received Jesus into your heart as Lord and Saviour, you believe that Jesus died on the cross for your sins, was buried, and rose again from the grave, and is alive *now* and in your heart as *King.* If you are sure of your salvation check here [ ].

14. Are you *now* a child of God, having received Jesus, who is life eternal? ....

If you have never yielded yourself to Jesus, why not now, in humility, surrender yourself to Him as Lord and Master? He took your sins in His own body on the cross. Jesus says, "Behold I stand at the door [of your heart], and knock: if any man hear my voice, and open the door, *I will come in to him*" (Rev. 3:20).

We would like to give you Lesson 2 of this Bible Study series. Please *print* your name and address and return to the person who gave you this study, or return to..........
.... Church,
Your name .... Address ....
....

PERSONAL BIBLE INVESTIGATION COURSE
GOSPEL OF JOHN SERIES

Lesson 2 — Jesus Christ, The Lord

We are so happy that you are going on with your Bible study. Remember to answer each question from the Scripture reference given in the Gospel of John, using your *own words*.

This lesson teaches us some of the things Jesus actually said about Himself and His relation to the Father, what others said about Him, and how we may know for sure that we have life eternal.

1. How may we come to know Jesus Christ in a personal way? (John, 5:39) ....
....
2. Who does Jesus say wrote about Him? (5:45-47) .....
3. What was John's *main* testimony about Jesus?? (1:34)
....
....
4. A greater witness than John's is .... (5:36-37)
5. What does Jesus say about those who claim to honor God, but do not honor the Son? (5:23; 8:18-19) ....

. . . .

6. What was Jesus really saying in calling God His Father? (5:17-18) . . . .

. . . .

7. Why did they seek to kill Jesus? (10:30-33) . . . .

. . . .

8. Jesus claimed to be (a) 30 years of age. (b) ageless and eternal. (c) about the same age as Abraham. (8:56-59; encircle correct answer) .

9. How has God personally revealed Himself to man? (14:6-9) . . . .

. . . .

10. If we come to Jesus, will He forsake us? (6:37) . . . .

11. What does a person *have,* who sincerely believes in Jesus? (6:47)

. . . .

12. What promise does He give to all who hear and believe Him? (10:27-29) . . . .

13. What three blessings are ours when we hear and believe Him? (5:24) . . . .

　　a. . . . .

　　b. . . . .

　　c. . . . .

14. If you were to die today, would you go to be with Jesus? . . . .

How do you know? . . . .

Have you taken Jesus' promise in 3:18, 36 as your own?

. . . .

If you are still not clear on salvation or assurance, please check here [ ].

Please return this lesson to the address below. You will receive it back, graded, by return mail, together with your next lesson. *Do it now!*

. . . . Church, ...

Your name . . . . Address. . . . .

. . . .

PERSONAL BIBLE INVESTIGATION COURSE
GOSPEL OF JOHN SERIES

Lesson 3 — The Abundant Life

Your continued faithfulness in these simple studies indicates a heart that God will surely bless abundantly. "Blessed are they which do hunger and thirst after righteousness, for they shall be filled" (Matt. 5:6).

Meeting Christ and receiving Him as Lord and Saviour of your life may take but a moment of time, but *getting to know Him* is a matter of growth in fellowship through the Bible, prayer, and fellowship in church. Sin is the only thing that blocks our union and communion with Jesus.

Remember to use *your own words as you prayerfully* "search the Scriptures" for His answer to the questions in this lesson.

1. Why did God send Jesus to us? (John 3:17) . . . .
. . . .

2. What is the result of Jesus' coming into our lives and being saved? (10:10b) *
. . . .

3. If we are to live abundantly, what new change does Jesus expect in our lives? (8:11) . . . .
. . . .

4. How is this change brought about? (15:3) . . . .
. . . .
. . . .

5. If His Word is going to change us, what must we do? (2:22) . . . .
. . . .
(Faith is coming to God and taking Him at His Word on what He has said).

6. What is truth? (14:6; 17:17) . . . .
. . . .

7. What does Jesus promise those who "know" the truth? (8:32) . . . .

. . . .

8. If we actively believe the Scriptures, from what may we expect freedom and over what victory? (8:34-36)

. . . .

9. What *new* promise belongs to those who believe and follow Christ? (14:13) . . . .

. . . .

10. What are God's conditions for answered prayer?
    a. John 15:7 . . . .
    b. John 15:13; 16:23 . . . .
    c. John 9:31 . . . .
    *The "b" refers to the last part of the verse (question 2).

It is God's desire that "your joy may be full" by answering your prayers. Have you asked and received a *specific* answer to prayer in the last month? . . . .

Attach a specific prayer request that is on your heart to one of the above promises from the Bible, then pray about it until you truly believe that God has heard you and will answer it. *Nothing* can take the place of a specific time for daily communion with God. One help in prayer is the "prayer list." Write down the names of your friends and relatives, your pastor and your church, and unsaved contacts. Ask *specific* things from God for them, and believe Him for great answers.

Your name . . . . Address . . . .

PERSONAL BIBLE INVESTIGATION COURSE
GOSPEL OF JOHN SERIES

Lesson 4 — The Disciple

A disciple is a follower and a learner. Jesus never looked for converts, only disciples. His command to the disciples was to "go into all the world and make disciples of all nations." This was His last earthly command! It takes a disciple to win and build another disciple for Jesus. This study will aid you in finding His will for your life in discipling men for Jesus. Be sure to answer each question, using your *own* words, after prayerful meditation on the verses given.

The true disciple—the marks of reality.

    1. What are the marks of a true disciple of Jesus Christ?
       (1:37) ....
       (8:31) ....
       (13:34-35) ....
    2. What, therefore, is the heart's prayer of every true disciple? (3:30) ....
       ....

The obedient disciple—the marks of responsiveness.

    3. Who is truly a friend of the Lord Jesus? (15:14) .....
    4. If a man truly loves the Lord, what two things will he *do* with Christ's commands? (14:21) ....
       and ....
    5. Why is it that many so-called converts never become true disciples of Christ? (12:42-43) ....
       ....

The fruitful disciple — the marks of relationship.

    6. What can we, in ourselves, do for the Lord Jesus? (15:5)
       ....
    7. What does the Good Shepherd promise His sheep which He leads? (10:4) ....
    8. Fruit is the natural result of (15:5) ....
    9. When Andrew met Jesus, what three things did he do? (1:40-42)
       a. ....
       b. ....
       c. ....
  10. Where are we sent? (17:18) ....
       Why? (15:16) ....
  11. What two things are necessary for the care of those who are new in the faith? (13:1) ....
       (21:16) ....

12. How may we be treated if we follow our Lord? (15:18-20) ....
....

13. What happens to everyone who does not accept Christ as Lord? (3:18; 8:24) ....
Do you believe that? .... Then have you personally witnessed of the living Saviour to any during the past thirty days? ....

Sin, ignorance, laziness, and fear can keep us from consistently winning others to Jesus. If you have been fruitless, why not confess it now and ask Christ to lead you to someone who needs Him. Fruit is excess life, the daily overflow of the life of Christ through us. Daily spending time in prayer and Bible study, together with consistent memorizing of scripture, is a basic essential for Spirit-led witnessing.

Your name .... Address.................

PERSONAL BIBLE INVESTIGATION COURSE
GOSPEL OF JOHN SERIES

Lesson 5 — Claiming the Promises

A promise is "one's pledge to another to do or not to do what is specified." God has placed in the Bible over 3,000 "pledges" to do. Some of His promises are conditioned on specific obedience; others are unconditional. But all must be *claimed by faith* to receive their blessings. To claim is "to demand as due." There are over sixty promises in the Gospel of John. Some of the most wonderful are listed in this study.

Carefully look up the references, write the answer *in your own words* — then prayerfully examine your own life in the light of each promise. Are you *now* believing it and using it in your daily life?

Promises to Believers:

1. Jesus makes three wonderful promises to all who hear His Word and believe.
   What are they? (John 5:24) a. ....

    b. ....

    c. ....

2. List some of the blessings to be claimed by those who truly believe in Him. (8:51; 11:26) ....

    (12:46) ....

    (15:5, 16) ....

    (16:33) ....

3. Where is Jesus and what three things does He promise us? (14:2-3)

    a. ....

    b. ....

    c. ....

Promises to Obedient Believers:

4. What is Jesus' promise to those who serve Him as their Lord? (12:26)

....

5. If we do what Jesus asks, two promises may be claimed from Him.

    Name them. (14:23) ....

    and ....

6. The greatest treasures are priceless. What does Jesus freely give to those who claim these promises? (a) (14:27) : ....

    (b) (10:11, 15) : ....

    (c) (15:9) : ....

7. If we faithfully practice what Jesus says, we have His

....

in us *now* (15:11).

Promises About the Holy Spirit:

8. Who comes as a "river of living water" to *all* who believe? (7:38-39)

We must remember, however, that the blessed Holy Spirit is *not* a liquid to fill an empty vessel. He is a *Person* who controls all who believe and will yield themselves to Him. Let us seek to know Him through the Scriptures and obey His leadings. "For as many as are led by the Spirit of God, they are the sons of God" (Rom. 8:14).

9. Since the Holy Spirit is given to all who believe in Jesus, what is His promise? (14:16) ....
How long will He stay in us? ....

10. What is the first work of the Spirit in anyone's life? (16:8) ....
....

11. What does He promise to do in the believer? (16:13)
....

12. Jesus promises happiness to those who ...... (13:17).

13. What verse in this study will you prayerfully believe *now* and claim for your life? ....

"For all the promises of God, in him are yea, and in him Amen, unto the glory of God by us" (II Cor. 1:20).

Your name .... Address ....

PERSONAL BIBLE INVESTIGATION COURSE
GOSPEL OF JOHN SERIES

Lesson 6 — Meditation

Meditation on the Word of God is perhaps the most neglected single spiritual avenue of blessing that Christians have today. It is the doorway to the application of the great truths of the Bible to our hearts. Meditation has been called "reflective thinking with a view to application." Two of God's greatest promises are conditioned on meditation. Look up Psalm 1:2-3 and Joshua 1:8.

The suggestions below will help you "break down" a verse or thought so that it can be grasped, and applied to your own life. This is the real purpose of the Bible — to change us into *Christians,* to be like Christ.

1. Choose one of these verses for your meditation: John 14:21; John 15:5; John 16:24; John 16:33. Circle the verse chosen. Now, read half a dozen verses before and

after the verse you have chosen. See every verse in its Scripture setting.

2. Write out the verse in your own words — make yourself rethink just what the verse says in the natural way you would say it, or paraphrase it to another person. *Do not copy it.* ....
....
....
....

3. Answer these questions about the verse. Write out any part that fits your verse. Not every question suits every verse listed above. Use your own words everywhere.

a. What *one* or *two* words in this verse seem to you to be the most important or basic? ....

b. Does this verse have:

   (1) A PROMISE TO CLAIM AND BELIEVE? (If so, what?) ....
   ....

   (2) A COMMAND TO OBEY AND FOLLOW? (Any condition for its being answered?) ....
   ....

   (3) A BLESSING FROM GOD TO THANK HIM FOR? ....
   ....

c. Why do I need this verse in my life? ....

d. What does this verse teach me for my life? ....
   ....

4. Prayerfully think through on how you can use this verse in your life *now*. (To meet a personal need, help a friend, believe God, increase prayer, witness, etc.) Write down what you will *do* with this verse in your life this week. Be specific, personal, and pointed.
   I will ....
   ....

"Meditate upon these things; give thyself wholly to them; that thy profiting may appear to all" (I Tim. 4:15).

Your name (please print)................................

Address ....

PERSONAL BIBLE INVESTIGATION COURSE
(JUNIOR GRADED)
GOSPEL OF JOHN SERIES

Lesson 1 — The Savior and Eternal Life

Giving yourself to Jesus Christ is the most important step you can take. But this is just the start of a wonderful new life with God. It is God's desire that you do four things: *Read* your Bible every day. Begin with this study to learn the Bible. *Pray* to God every day, thanking Jesus for your salvation; confess any sin to Him and ask His Spirit to guide you. *Witness* for Jesus at school, at home, and at play by showing others that your life is new and that Jesus dwells inside you. *Go to church* every week. Do not miss Sunday school. Bring some friend along with you if you can. Tell others about your Saviour and your church.

Here is your first Bible study lesson. To answer the questions, please follow directions. Use the Gospel of John to answer each question.

Turn to the Verse Listed, Then Fill in the Blanks.

1. John 20:31 — The Gospel of John was "written, that ye .... that Jesus is the Christ, the ...... of God."
2. John 5:39 — We find the truth about Jesus as "we ".......... ...."
3. John 1:29 — John called Jesus the .... of ...... because He would .... away the ...... of the world. Only sin keeps you from God. Jesus died to take our sins away, and bring us to God.

Encircle the Number That Gives the Best Answer.

4. Who is going to heaven and has eternal life? (John 17:3) (1) A good person who tries hard. (2) One who

is baptized. (3) One who knows Jesus by trusting Him as his Saviour.

5. God let His Son Jesus die on the cross for you because: (John 3:16)

(1) He loves you. (2) He couldn't stop the people from killing Jesus. (3) He wants you to remember how nice Jesus was.

Using John 3:16, Fill in the Blanks Below:

"For God so .... the world [that means you] that he .... his .... begotten ...."
Jesus Christ came to earth from heaven to die on the cross for you and take your sins away.

Put your first name on the following dotted lines: "For God so loved .... that he gave his only begotten Son, that if .... believes in him, ... should not perish, but .... should have everlasting life."

Circle the word in John 1:12 that means the same as to "believe" in Jesus: (1) power; (2) receive; (3) Son. Have you received Jesus as your own Saviour, inviting Him into your heart? If the answer is "yes," be sure and thank Him in prayer for dying for you and living in your heart now. If you have not yet received Jesus as your Saviour, check here ....

Now hand in this study soon and you will get Lesson 2 with your grade on this study.

Your name (please print) ....

Address ....

PERSONAL BIBLE INVESTIGATION COURSE (JUNIOR GRADED)

GOSPEL OF JOHN SERIES

Lesson 2 — Jesus Christ, the Lord

Good for you! We are so happy that you did your Lesson 1. See how well you can do on this second lesson. Remember to look up the Scripture reference given in the Gospel of John, then carefully answer each question in your *own* words. Do *not* just copy the answer from the Bible. Keep on digging into the Bible.

1. What has God given to us, to teach us about Jesus? (John 5:39) ....
   Do you read it daily? ....

2. Who does Jesus say wrote about Him (5:45-47) ......

3. What did John the Baptist say about Jesus (1:34) ....
   ....

4. Fill in the blanks below after looking up the Scriptures.
   a. John 5:23 — Jesus said, "That .... men should .... the Son, even as they honour the Father. He that honoureth not the .... honoureth not the Father which hath ...."

   b. John 5:18 — When Jesus called God His Father the people tried to kill Him, "Because he not only hàd broken the sabbath, but .... also that God ...., making himself ...."

Choose and encircle the number of the best answer.

5. People tried to stone Jesus because: (John 10:33)
   a. He did good things.
   b. He made Himself equal to God.
   c. He was a bad man.

6. Jesus said He was: (John 8:57-58) a. 30 years old.
   b. Ageless; before Abraham. c. As old as Abraham.

7. God has shown us what He is like by: (John 14:8-9)
   a. Painted pictures of Himself.
   b. The sun and moon and trees.
   c. Jesus, who is God's love-gift.

8. Receiving Jesus into your heart as Saviour and believing on Him means you now have: (John 6:47; 10:10)
   a. Everlasting, abundant life. b. A hope of heaven.
   c. The same old life.

Fill in the missing words from John 10:28.

    9. Jesus says, "I .... unto them ....
and they shall .... perish, neither shall ....
.... pluck them out of ...." Are
you trusting in Jesus as your Saviour? ....
  10. Then, if you were to die today, would you go to be
with Jesus? ....
How do you know? ....
  11. Have you believed Jesus as your Saviour from the
penalty of sin? .... If you are still not sure of
eternal life and heaven, check here .... Also
look up John 3:18, 36. Have you truly believed?....

Your name (please print) ....

Address ....

HOME BIBLE STUDY

You and Your Church

Please open your Bible to the reference, writing the
answer to each question in your *own* words. Ask God for
wisdom as you study.

    1. To what has the believer been called? I Corinthians,
chapter 1, verse 9 (I Cor. 1:9) ....
    2. What other blessings come to us from fellowship to-
gether in church?
        a. Jeremiah 3:15 ....
        b. Matthew 18:19 ....
        c. Psalm 27:4 ....
        d. Colossians 3:16 ....
        e. Psalm 29:2 ....
    3. What then should be our response to the opportunity
of fellowship in the church? Psalm 122:1 ....
Not only does the church minister to Christians, but
it also is God's channel for service to others. You will
find many opportunities for the use of your God-given
spiritual gifts and resources through the church.

4. List some of the different gifts with which members of the church may serve one another. Remember, you have at least *one* spiritual gift. (Romans 12:3-8)

a. .... b. ....

c. .... d. .... e. ....

f. .... g. ....

5. Church membership and attendance alone are not substitutes for active participation. List some of the opportunities for service in your church as recorded in Acts 6:1-4: ....

....,

6. A Christian in full fellowship with the Lord and His church will:

a. Acts 8:36-37 ....

b. James 1:22 ....

c. Romans 15:1; Galatians 6:2 ....

d. I Corinthians 4:2; Luke 6:38 ....

e. Acts 8:4; 4:20 ....

7. How should this service be performed? (Eph. 6:6; Col. 3:23) ....

....

8. What was the last command of Christ? (Matthew 28: 19-20) ....

....

To whom was the order given? (28:17-18) ....

9. We are to be His disciples, too. What things prove a person to be His disciple? John 8:31 ....

John 13:34-35 ....

John 15:8 ....

10. Which question in this study has helped you the most? ....

Why? ....

Your name (please print) ....

Address ....

HOME BIBLE STUDY

Walking in Victory

Please fill in each blank prayerfully in your *own words*.

1. What has been given to every believer through Jesus Christ? (I Cor. 15:57) ....
....

2. Though victory is promised, who is our chief enemy? (I Peter 5:8) ....
What are some other names and occupations of the devil? (II Cor. 11:14) : ....
(II Cor. 4:4) : .... (Rev. 12:10) : ....
(Luke 22:31) : .... (I Cor. 5:5) : ....

3. Because we are Christians does this free us from his temptations? (II Cor. 2:11) ....

4. What three avenues does he use to tempt us to sin? (I John 2:15-16) ....
....

5. Temptations come from .... (Jas. 1:14)

6. Does God tempt us in any way? (Jas. 1:13) ....

7. Since God permits temptation to come our way, what value is it to the believer? (Jas. 1:2-4) ....

8. What four things does God say about temptation? (I Cor. 10:13)
   a. ....   b. ....
   c. ....   d. ....

9. When tempted, what are we to do? (Jas. 4:7) ....
....

10. What weapon has God made available to defeat Satan and to escape the pressures of temptation? (Eph. 6:17)
....

11. Jesus met the attack of Satan's temptations through
....
(Matt. 4:4, 7, 10)

12. As members of Christ's church, against what special temptations must we guard? (Heb. 12:14-15) ....
(Heb. 13:17) ....

(James 2:8-9) ....
13. If we fall into temptation, what must we immediately
    do for restoration of fellowship with our Holy God?
    (I John 1:9) ....
    ....
14. Victory is in a Person, the Lord Jesus. He indwells the
    believer to meet all temptations in victory as we, mo-
    ment by moment, yield to the Spirit's control. How is
    this way of victory described by Paul?
    (Rom. 13:14) ....
    (Gal. 5:16) ....
    (Eph. 5:18) ....
    The Holy Spirit is a Person, to control (fill) each
    believer moment by moment. There must be a conscious
    yielding to and dependence upon the Holy Spirit to
    work His victory in our hearts. Then how must we
    walk each day? (II Cor. 5:7) ....
    (Heb. 10:38) ....
15. Which verse in this study will you claim and apply,
    today? ....
    How? ....

Your name (please print)   ....
Address ....

"Study the Scriptures" Bible Study

The "Study the Scriptures" study (p. 163) is flexible, designed to meet the needs of a wide variety of people with
varying abilities and opportunities for study. An entire chapter, a portion of a chapter, or a single verse may be studied
at one time.

First, "What does it say?" It is always important when
studying the Scriptures to read carefully what is written.
Direct your attention first to the actual contents rather than
to the interpretation of the passage. You may write out a summary, or you may prefer to outline what the chapter says.

A *summary* is, as the word suggests, a brief résumé of the

chapter. Care should be taken to include all parts of the chapter in proper balance, not giving too much space to one part and overlooking another. It should include all the important points and must be briefly yet clearly stated in your own words.

One way is to summarize each paragraph of the chapter, using synonyms for the words of the text and making the summary as long as necessary to be complete. Then go through the summary and condense it into fewer words, bringing it down to an average of five to eight words per verse. Don't try to summarize verse by verse, but by thoughts or paragraphs. Add your total words at the end (for instance, 20 verses $\times$ 8 $=$ 160, the maximum number of words in your summary).

If you do an *outline,* divide the chapter into natural divisions or paragraphs, giving a brief title or heading to each one and noting the verses each includes. List as many subpoints under each of these main headings as are needed to define its contents. Do not give too much space to one part of the chapter or portion and overlook another part. All important points should be included.

Second, "What does it say I don't understand?" Read through the passage slowly and see if you can explain everything. Record with the verse reference anything you are unable to explain or answer satisfactorily. State the problem clearly and briefly. After you have noted the problems you cannot answer fully, list the possible problems others may have in answering.

Third, "What does it say to me?" The heart of Bible study is its practical application to your life. This is the most important aspect of the study. In writing what the Scripture says to you, use the personal, singular pronouns "I," "me," etc. An application should be practical, concerned with truth which may be translated into your daily life. It should be stated clearly enough to be understood by anyone you might ask to read it. The application may be drawn from a verse or group of verses that develop one particular thought. Write the verse number (s) at the beginning of each application.

You may formulate a profit either on your relation to God or on your relation to man. When applied, the profit will either result in personal spiritual enrichment and up-lifting by deepening your devotion to the Lord or improve your relationship to fellow Christians or those outside of Christ. You may draw the profit from a promise, a command, or some truth that speaks to your own heart.

In formulating your profit or application you may find these suggestions helpful:

1. State in your own words the truth of the verse or verses from which you draw your application.

2. Indicate how this applies to you — what needs this brings out in your life, where you fall short, or what new appreciation or understanding it gives.

3. Write what you intend to do about it — what definite action you intend to take now to correct the weakness, build the needed quality into your life, strengthen your understanding, etc. Sometimes the step to be taken may be memorizing a verse on the subject, or making a special study of it, or praying especially about the need. It may be writing a letter of apology, righting some wrong done by doing some kindness. Whatever the action, it is well to be specific as to your intent, and to make some provision to carry it out. It is good to provide some way to refer back to see that you have followed through on the action.

Optional: "What does it say in other places?" You will best understand a portion of Scripture as you allow other passages to throw light on it. Read each verse or passage carefully, then meditate on it and try to remember one or more good cross-references for that particular passage. These may be drawn from verses you have memorized, or familiar chapters. If your memory fails to produce a good cross-reference, use a concordance or the margin of your Bible to find one. It is important to try to find a cross-reference for the *thought* of the verse, rather than to select verses which merely use an identical word.

In the place marked "Reference" put the book, chapter and verse reference. In the column to the right put down the key thought or idea in the verse that makes it a good cross-reference. This enables you to refer quickly to all your passages.

Use the back of the study sheet to complete any of the points.

Group Use of "Study the Scriptures"

When using the "Study the Scriptures" study with a group of Christians with varying degrees of understanding and time for study, it is well to go through a book of the Bible a chapter at a time. Those who have the time and ability can study the entire chapter according to the "Study the Scriptures" plan. Those who have less time for study or who are without sufficient background in methods of Bible study may use the same form to concentrate on what they consider the most important portion of the chapter. This may include a few verses, half the chapter, or even more. It may be, however, that the group as a whole will decide to take the key verse or a portion of a chapter as their basis for study.

If the above plan is followed, no one should ever have to come to a class or a group discussion in which this study is being used without having some work done. This is particularly valuable to the one who, if he failed to complete his work over a period of time, would ordinarily become discouraged and drop out. When one is given this choice of varying amounts which he can consider a completed study, he is far more likely to become consistent in Bible study than he would if the same amount of study were required from all who attend. It is very important that those doing the "Study the Scriptures" study do something each week, whether it be the entire chapter, a portion, or the key verse. Steady progress builds the kind of habits that will soon enable a person to finish a whole chapter each time. It is better to have a smaller group, with definite standards set, than a larger group of students who come together unprepared to share personal study blessings.

Completing the study of an average-size chapter should take between two and three hours in weekly preparation, but better study habits are built by spending 20 to 30 minutes each day on the unit. A class that sets the standard of a completed chapter a week should expect only the most diligent disciples, with a "built-in" devotional life, to keep up. This study will definitely tell the pastor who is willing to mean business, and whether a person is ready for advanced study.

Conducting "Study the Scriptures" Groups

A leader should be in charge, who must direct the amount of time spent on each section of the study. He will normally be the most advanced layman in the group, or the pastor. Discussion time should average one hour per week. All four sections may be covered on the night of the meeting, or special emphasis may be given to one or two sections.

For discipling men, the pastor should require completed studies and should check on each man at the weekly meeting for finished work. Those having trouble should be given personal help and encouragement. This study should be given only to individuals who have completed a number of the question-answer studies and who evidence faithfulness in their daily time with God.

Short books of the New Testament can be studied after favorite passages and chapters. Many groups study one-half chapter a week when a chapter is over twenty verses. A suggested order: II Timothy 3:14-17; Philippians 4:4-9; Psalm 1, and then a short chapter like I Thessalonians 1 or I John 1.

The leader takes up study sheets each week and must keep accurate records on personal application. The study should be checked for neatness, clarity of thought, and pointedness of application to the student's life situation. Noting each student's application gives the leader private food for intercession.

(Pattern for "Study the Scriptures" printed or mimeographed
sheets)

Study the Scriptures
PASSAGE: .... DATE: ....
YOUR NAME ....
ENTITLE THE PASSAGE ....
I. WHAT DOES IT SAY?
II. WHAT DOES IT SAY I DON'T UNDERSTAND?
III. WHAT DOES IT SAY TO ME?

OPTIONAL:
IV. WHAT DOES IT SAY IN OTHER PLACES?

Verse	Reference	Short thought on verse
1.		
2.		
3.		
4.		
5.		
6.		
7.		
8.		

(Use back of page for further writing)

Scripture Memory

One thing we must make time for in this busy world of ours is the Bible. Busy people have found Scripture memory the most profitable and useful way to gain a knowledge of the Bible from key verses. Billy Graham has said, "I believe that regular, systematic memorization of Scripture is one of the most effective means of growth for a Christian. I recommend it to pastors, businessmen, professional people, everyone, as a rich source of blessing for their lives." Why memorize? Consistent Scripture memorizing will provide these definite blessings for your life:

1. It helps you to know Jesus Christ and to love Him more fully.
2. It enables you to walk in victory over sin and temptation. Jesus used Scripture as a weapon to defeat Satan in the wilderness (Matt. 4:1—11). This experience is told as an example for *us* to follow.
3. It prepares you for a life of spiritual growth and obedience (I Pet. 2:2; Deut. 30:14).
4. It aids and enlarges your ability to study and to teach the Bible (Col. 3:16). Through memory you will be able to compare Scripture with Scripture (Isa. 28:9-10).
5. It helps you find related passages elsewhere in Scripture. For example, Acts 27:25 (on faith) recalls the "shipwreck chapter."
6. It makes us "ready to give an answer to every man . . ." (I Pet. 3:15). A prepared heart is a heart filled with the Word (Ps. 119:41-42).
7. It is invaluable for personal witnessing. Nothing can take the place of a "thus saith the Lord" by showing chapter and verse in witnessing. All soul-winners use some memorized verses for ready reference.
8. It guides you into a knowledge of God's will for you. Scriptures hidden in the heart shed light on daily decisions (Ps. 119:105). They reprove and say, "This is the way, walk ye in it" (Isa. 30:21).
9. It gives you delight and joy through the day (Ps. 119:103; 19:8).
10. It is Scriptural. Jesus, the Apostles, and the writers of the New Testament quote verses and passages from the Old Testament. Stephen, a man "filled with the Holy Ghost," in Acts 7 quotes directly or indirectly over ninety Scripture portions from sixteen Old Testament books, from Genesis to Amos. The *example* of mighty men of God is ample reason.

How to memorize: Memorize to get the basic principle from a given verse, from God's mind to yours, with a view to application. Routine memory without application is a deadening thing. But ignorance of basic Scripture verses over a period of time is just as bad. Both defects make people limited in their service to Christ. Be *systematic* and *consistent* in your memorization. Start with two or three verses per week. Put Scriptures on cards for carrying with you during the day. *Review* is the secret to successful memory. Use it or lose it. Once memorized, a verse should be carefully turned over in the mind with a thought to personal application.

What to memorize: Some memorize the key verse of each chapter they study. Certainly verses on soul-winning should be a part of any memory program. Basic doctrinal verses should also be learned, because Satan will fight anyone who consistently seeks to inscribe God's Word on the tables of his heart.

Helps in memory: The Navigators, Box 1861, Colorado Springs, Colorado, have for over twenty-two years helped multiplied thousands through to victory in Scripture memory. Their Topical Memory System Correspondence Course ($3.00) is unreservedly recommended by the author.

Verse-a-Day Meditation

Meditation is the doorway to application of the truths of the Word to our hearts. It has been called "reflective thinking" with a view to application. Two of the greatest promises in the Bible make meditation the condition for their fulfillment in our lives: Joshua 1:8 and Psalm 1:2-3. All of us spend specific time in hearing the Word; many read the Word daily; a few study and memorize consistently; but very few people ever spend a *definite* daily time in meditation. The suggestions below are designed to aid you in the "how" of breaking down a verse or thought from the Scripture, that your life may be "changed, from glory to glory, even as by the Spirit of the Lord" (II Cor. 3:18):

1. Single out a truth to meditate on; start with one verse. Check the verse in its context; read at least five or six verses before and after the verse.

2. Paraphrase the verse; get it down in your *own* words. Write it out if you are at home; say it aloud if you travel.

3. Emphasize different words in the verse aloud, by exclamation. Example: "*I* can do all things...I *can* do all things...I can *do* all things," etc.

4. Ask yourself questions about the verse: How? What? Where? Why? When? Let these words enable you to turn the verse around and around, seeing it from many viewpoints, always with your own personal application in mind. In this verse is there a promise to claim (any conditions?), or an example to follow, or a command to obey, or something to praise God for?

5. Seek an immediate personal application of a truth in the verse to your life *now*. How do you need the verse and Why?

    a. Think of some lack of application of the truth recently.

    b. What do you plan to do about this need this week? Example: John 16:24 — prayer in Jesus' name. Possible specific application might be: (1) to spend each day at least fifteen minutes in prayer, asking one definite thing in Jesus' name; (2) to have my wife, friends, or husband check me on what definite answers to prayer I am getting.

    Fight haziness in your applications: Satan deals in generalities; the Holy Spirit deals in specifics.

Many will find that these suggestions work well with a memory verse. If you memorize, say, three verses per week, you may enjoy meditating on the first verse the day after you memorize it. Then the next day memorize a new verse and the day following meditate on it.

APPENDIX B

ILLUSTRATIONS FOR TEACHING

The Wheel Illustration: The Christ-centered, Spirit-filled, fruitful life.[1]

Our physical bodies require certain things for living and growth: food, air, rest, and exercise. Without these four in proper balance we become unhealthy; we may stop growing, or become sick, or even die.

Spiritually, certain things are also necessary in order to be rightly related to Christ. God wants all of us to become mature (Col. 1:28; Eph. 4:13, 15). Maturity is a matter of spiritual growth. We use the illustration of a wheel to demonstrate the Christian living his life, *in this world,* in proper relationship to His Lord and to his fellow men.

The Christian is represented by the rim of the wheel (the rim may be drawn before class). He is in contact with the world (draw a line under and touching the bottom of the wheel). He is "in the world, but not of the world."

Every wheel has a center; every person living has a central thing in his life. Sometimes it is a job, or the family, or some recreation. For the believer, only one thing can be central if he is to grow and live a fruitful Christian life.

The Center of the Christian life is Christ (print CHRIST in the hub). It is the purpose of the wheel to move forward in response to the power and direction which comes from the hub. Smooth and steady progress is possible only when Christ is central in our lives. The very heart of the wheel in action is the hub, which furnishes the driving power as well as being

1 Wheel diagram used by permission of The Navigators.

167

the point upon which the wheel is centered and balanced. Christ must replace every other thing in the life of the believer or else the believer's walk is paralyzed, his testimony dulled; and he ceases to function in the purpose for which he was made by God.

In order to give us a completely different kind of life from anyone else in the world, God has done two wonderful things for those who have trusted in His Son (there are many others, but the two mentioned below form a basis for the believer's new relationship and growth in grace) :

First, there is the *life in Christ* (II Cor. 5:17; Col. 2:6, 9-10; give the references). God the Holy Spirit has placed us in a wonderful position, actually *in* Christ. Think of what this truth can mean in our daily life, in times of trouble, amid pressure and trial.

Secondly, Christ is our *life*. He is our center; He is *in* us; we have been invaded! Many verses tell us of this amazing truth: John 15:5; Philippians 1:6; Galatians 2:20; II Corinthians 13:5. The resource of the Christian life is Christ Himself! Christ is our life; this is a literal, actual truth. He has taken us into union with Himself by living in us. In Philippians 1:21, Paul does not say, "For me to live is to imitate Christ" or, "For me to live is to have Christ as a helper", nor even, "To me to live is to be Christlike." He says, "To me to live . . . *is* Christ!" "He therefore does not want us to work for Him, He wants us to let Him do His work through us, using us as we use a pencil to write with — better still, using us as one of the fingers of His hand. When our life is not only Christ's, but Christ Himself, our life will be a willing life, a serving life," says C. G. Trumbull in "The Life That Wins."

God has also given us, however, certain "spokes" which help us keep Christ at our center. There are at least four major spokes which give balance to the life of Christ. (Draw the spokes and ask the class to name four things that are necessary to teach each new baby for the baby's physical growth and health.) A baby must learn how to eat, talk, walk, and share; or, how to assimilate the Bible, pray, obey, and witness.

E A T   (Matt. 4:4; I Pet. 2:2; Acts 20:32; Jer. 15:16; II Tim. 3:16, 17; Col. 3:16)

Every Christian must learn to eat the Word of God regularly. It is spiritual food. First someone feeds us; later we learn to feed ourselves, then grow to maturity, learning to feed others. Many Christians jump from being fed to feeding others, without learning to feed themselves. Explain the parallel of eating daily to studying the Bible daily. Eating a spiritual banquet once a week on Sunday does not nourish the believer like daily spiritual food.

The Bible is a "spiritual supermarket." It contains 31,000 verses, or canned goods, packages, and frozen foods. There is food for every spiritual need. The believer must develop ability to select his own food, then prepare and eat it; eventually he grows in experience so that he can serve tasty meals of God's Word to others.

T A L K   (John 16:24; Matt. 21:22; Hebrews 4:15, 16; I John 5:14, 15; Ps. 66:18; Prov. 28:9)

Talking to God in prayer coupled with eating the Word are the two major *intake* spokes of the Wheel. A child does not talk automatically; he must hear others. Prayer is caught as well as taught. God urgently desires communication in worship with us. He seeks us to worship Him in prayer (John 4:23). The five basic kinds of prayer are adoration or praise, thanksgiving, intercession, petition, and confession. Teach the need for a "Quiet Time."

W A L K   (John 14:21; 15:10, 14; Hebrews 5:8, 9; Gen. 22:18; II Cor. 5:7; Amos 3:3)

We learn to walk physically a step at a time. To walk spiritually is to obey the Lord. A life of obedience to God's will is but a series of steps. Walking is Paul's word for the normal life of a believer in Christ (Eph. 2:10; 4:1, 17; 5:2, 8, 15). It is normal for the growing child to walk; it is tragic when he does not walk. Disobedience paralyzes the Christian life. Yielding moment by moment to the Spirit enables the believer to have an effective Christlike walk.

S H A R E   (I John 1:3; I Peter 3:15; Acts 1:8; Matt. 28:19, 20; Acts 22:15)

Selfishness and self-centeredness ruin a life. When a child is born, he is at the center of his universe. As his awareness increases, he begins to understand that he has relationships and responsibilities to others. Effective witnessing is sharing our most precious possession, the living Christ; it is to live unselfishly before others. We witness by the way we live as well as by what we say. Witnessing can be, therefore, both positive and negative. Effective sharing is the overflow of a personal love relationship with Christ. Obedience and witnessing are the *output* spokes of the wheel. The teacher will want to show the class the difference between "the Gospel" (I Cor. 15:3, 4), a "testimony" (Acts 26:3-30), and "soulwinning" (Prov. 11:30; Jas. 5:19-20). The Spirit using a believer to bring a person to the place of surrender to Christ and His will could be termed "soulwinning."

Notice how each of the spokes depends upon all the others, and how each depends upon your intake of the Word. Without consistent intake of the Word and prayer, there will not be effective output of the believer's life in obedience and witnessing. (The teacher should withdraw one spoke, then another, showing the interrelationship of all four, emphasizing how they all break down unless each spoke is firmly in place.)

The Holy Spirit. Many will ask, "Haven't you omitted the Holy Spirit in the spokes of the wheel?" No, because the Holy Spirit is in every phase of the Christian life, and is indispensable. The following verses will show the relationship which the Holy Spirit has to every part of the Wheel illustration.

In salvation — John 3:5, 8
In our putting Christ first — John 16:14
In teaching us the Word — John 14:26
In prayer — Romans 8:26-27
In obedience — Galatians 5:25
In personal witnessing — Acts 1:8

The Holy Spirit, the agent of salvation, places us into Christ. Then at the same instant of salvation, He comes to dwell in us as His earthly house (I Cor. 6:19-20). We are His property; His home base of operations, through which He presents the Lord Jesus Christ to the world. There is no victorious life without being under His constant control. We are commanded to "be filled with the Spirit." The Greek word for "filled" is "controlled." He is a Person who controls us as we by faith yield moment-by-moment to Him. The Spirit-led man is always one in whose life all the spokes of the wheel are strongly placed. In such a life, Christ is central.

Bridge of Life Illustration

The "Bridge of Life" Illustration graphically represents sin separating man from God. As we develop the illustration, we can show the unsaved how they may become reconciled to God. One of the reasons God created man was to have unbroken fellowship with him. That fellowship was broken by sin. The illustration is numbered to show the order of its presentation. Do *not* number the parts when actually presenting it to the lost.

All one needs to present this illustration to the unsaved is something with which to write and a piece of paper — lunch sack, paper napkin, etc. You can give it anywhere, any time. Writing and drawing is non-offensive in public and gives opportunity for witnessing in places where a Bible might be conspicuous and embarrass the person you contact. Normally, the Bridge may be introduced by saying, "Here is an illustration which I came across recently that I think you might be very much interested in. It is about God and man. It will take

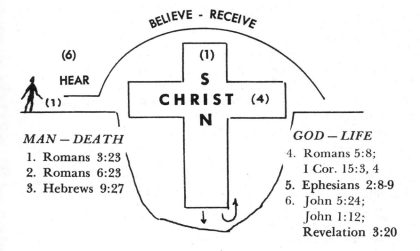

(For Teaching Personal Witnessing)

only a short time, but I know it will mean a lot to you, because it explains clearly something about our relationship with God which I never saw in this light before."

Sketch two cliffs with a wide gap between. Print MAN on the left side, and **GOD** on the right side. Draw a little line figure of a man on the left and say that we usually associate man with death because he doesn't live long; he always dies. We associate God with life, because He is eternal. Print "Death" by "Man" and "Life" by "God." The stick figure represents the person with whom you are talking.

Now ask him, "Do you know what separates man from God? For centuries man has been trying to reach God and really know God, but something seems to block the way." Whatever his answer, say, "The Bible tells us what stands between us and God in Romans 3:23." Quote the verse slowly or read it from a small Testament. Then ask the contact such questions about the verse as, "What separates man from God?" "How many people have sinned?" "Does this mean you?" Always use questions after giving a verse so that you may know whether its truth is getting across. Giving him a verse doesn't mean he understands that verse; never take anything for granted in dealing with a soul. *All* men are lost, unless you have asked them and gotten an assured answer that they are His saved children.

1. Draw in S-I-N, showing that it separates man from God.

2. Then show that all sin pays is death (Rom. 6:23).

3. And that this death which is the penalty for sin ends in judgment (Heb. 9:27). Emphasize the death side of the picture.

Now begin to develop God's side and show that all is not hopeless. God's holiness refuses to receive anything sinful into His presence. God's justice requires the payment of death for sin, but the payment has been made.

4. God's love provided that payment, the bridge across the gap between sinful man and a holy God, by the death of His Son, Jesus Christ, on the cross, for man's sin. Draw a cross which bridges the gap between man's side and God's side. Because Christ was both man and God, He brought them together through Himself (Rom. 5:8).

Show that Christ became S-I-N itself (II Cor. 5:21) that we might have the "righteousness of God." The "I" in SIN should coincide with the "I" in CHRIST. Emphasize the substitution of Christ for us. Here it is vital to stress the heart of the gospel (I Cor. 15:3-4). Not only did Jesus die for our sins, but He was buried and arose from the grave on the third day. We serve a living Christ, not a baby in a manger or a dead man hanging on a cross! Stress that the fact of His death, burial, and resurrection is "according to the scriptures."

5. Now explain that man is not saved by what he tries to do, by himself, to get across the gap. Good works and sin-

cerity, baptism, church membership, or anything else, can never substitute for the Bridge which Christ Himself has become for us. Draw small bridges, putting on them the things you think your contact possibly is hiding behind for his salvation. Quote Ephesians 2:8-9 and help him to see that salvation is God's work, not man's.

6. Then tell the contact how one can pass from death to life according to John 5:24. One must first *hear,* then *believe.* Hearing is not enough. Show a line from the little figure to the edge of the cross — hearing will never get us any farther than that, just to the cross. Believing in Christ as personal Lord and Saviour takes us across the bridge of His cross to eternal life. Stress that the word "believe" doesn't mean mere mental assent. God has given us another word in John 1:12, which means the same thing as "to believe." By this time you may take out your Testament, if not before, and have him read this verse carefully and pick out the word that means the same as "believe" (receive). Show him that salvation is receiving a Person, Jesus Christ, as Lord and Master, into one's heart.

Revelation 3:20 is an excellent verse to show how Christ took the initiative. He it is who "knocks" on our heart's door, wanting to come in and save us. Notice the same idea in this verse as in John 5:24: "If any man *hear* my voice, and open the door [receive Him], I will come in to him." To "hear" means to realize our need for Christ, and to "open the door" means to trust Him as our Saviour, to be willing to yield ourselves completely to Him, accepting His death on the cross as payment for our own sins.

Next we ask vital, decision-provoking questions. One of the real problems in soul-winning is to help a person see that *this* is decision time, not a time to think about it. You have just presented to him all he ever needs to know in order to be saved. Prayerfully and carefully seek to point him to the need of an immediate decision. The following questions may also be used profitably in other situations such as after you have given a long testimony of your salvation or after you have taken an unsaved person to hear a gospel message. They should be memorized.

1. After we have presented our testimony, or the "Bridge Illustration," ask, "Does what I have said make sense to you?" or "Does this make sense to you?"

2. "Have you ever done anything about *it?*" The "it" is always your point of closing in on him. In the "Bridge Illustration" it is either "receiving Christ" or "opening the door of your heart."

3. "Is there any reason you know of why you can't do something about it?" Allow any objection to enter in here. Most objections are smoke screens, but ask this question as if there could not be any objection ever offered. Be always positive.

4. Then ask, "Wouldn't you like to do something about it *now?*" Or, "Wouldn't you like for Christ to come into your heart right now?" Expect the unsaved to respond! Remember, the center in his salvation is always his acceptance of Christ as Saviour, not what he doesn't like about the church, or his past sins, etc. *The* sin is unbelief (John 16:9).

Afterwards it is good to have a simple prayer. Suggest that if he is willing to trust Christ he should ask Him to come into his heart. If the unsaved says, "I don't know what to pray," then suggest that he simply say, "Thank you, Jesus, for dying on the cross for me and taking my sins. Come into my heart now. I give my life to You."

After this, you pray. Sometimes you have to lead a person in prayer, saying a sentence, then having him repeat it after you. Then use John 5:24 (p. 177) to help him with assurance. Note it indicates their past, present, and future state in Christ. The "I will" in Revelation 3:20 also aids in presenting assurance passages.

The Bridge of Life Assurance Illustration

Use this illustration after the "Bridge Illustration" to help new believers gain assurance. When they receive Christ, they

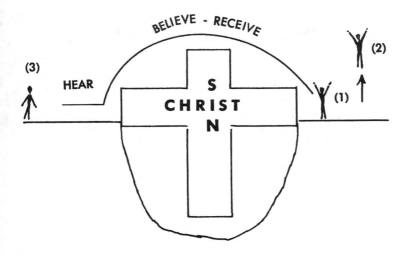

have everlasting life. This is their present state. Jesus promises that we *"shall not come* [future] into condemnation," but are "passed from death [our past state] unto life."

Go over the illustration, using Scripture until the person is trusting in what God says and not his own feelings. Do *not* tell the person he is saved! This is the work of the Holy Spirit through His Word.

John 5:24 — OUR ASSURANCE

1. "Hath everlasting life" — present state, now!

2. "Shall not come into condemnation" — future state, then.

3. ". . . passed from death unto life" — past state, when.

The Wordless Book

This five-color booklet has been an effective tool for children and young people's evangelism for over fifty years. An outstanding layman evangelist uses the Wordless Book with adult congregations with great success in conversions. It is taught in the Evangelism Class primarily as an illustrative help to a clear gospel presentation. The Wordless Book has proved itself as a means of helping children understand the basic doctrines of the gospel message; they can be taught to witness to their friends and schoolmates in a most effective way.

Introduction to the Wordless Book

I have here in my hands a little book which has no words in it, yet it tells the most wonderful story one could ever hear. Each page has a different color and a story all its own. This book without words tells us how much God loves us, and what He has done to make a happy home for us to live with Him. Would you like to hear the story?

The Gold Page — HEAVEN (A prepared place for a prepared person).

Do you know what the gold page stands for? It stands for heaven. Heaven is a real place. When the Lord Jesus left this earth He said that He was going to get a place ready for us, where we could be with Him forever (John 14:2-3). He has been preparing this place — heaven — for many, many years. It is more wonderful than anyone could ever dream. The Bible tells us some things about heaven, to give us an idea of a few things we will find there. Let us now remember:

1. What is *not* in heaven.
    a. No church (Rev. 21:22). Why? We go to church to worship God, but there we shall be with Him and see Him.
    b. No sun or moon (Rev. 21:23). Why? The glory of God is there, and the "light of the world," the Lord Jesus, is there, too.
    c. No night (Rev. 22:5). We will live in a place of endless daytime.
    d. No tears or sickness (Rev. 21:4). No death, either. There we will live forever.

    e. No sin (Rev. 21:27). Where God is, there is absolute purity and perfection. Sin would spoil heaven, so there is none there.

2. What *is* in heaven:

    a. God, upon His throne (Rev. 22:3). He loves us and wants us to be with Him in this wonderful place.

    b. The angels (Rev. 5:11). They will be our servants — and there are ten thousand times ten thousand angels there, and more.

    c. Those whose names are written in the Lamb's Book of Life (Rev. 21:27). Only those who have received Jesus will be there.

    d. Streets paved with gold (Rev. 21:19-21). So many beautiful things will be in heaven and it will be unlike anything we have ever seen.

    e. The Lord Jesus. We shall be with Him forever; we shall see His face, and the nail prints in His hands, and we shall talk and walk with our Saviour!

Isn't that a wonderful and beautiful place? Now, tell me, do you know *why* God made heaven? (Let some answer the question). The main reason God made heaven is that He *loves* us. He wants us to be with Him. He wants us to be happy and well and free from sickness and pain and death. One day all who love His Son, the Lord Jesus, will be with Him in heaven. Now, why did God make heaven? How many of you would like to go to this wonderful place when God calls for you? There is only *one* thing which will keep people from going to heaven, and that is S-I-N. (Turn to the black page).

Note: When the teacher mentions the "heart" it is well to make clear to children that you are not referring to the organ in their bodies, which is neither black nor white, but to what makes them what they are; their whole selves, inside. The heart is our real self which lives inside our body house. Since a child is so literal-minded, let us make sure we do *not* tell a child he has a black heart, but a sinful heart; neither does a child have a white heart, but a clean heart.

The Black Page — SIN

What is sin? Yes, sin makes us do wrong things. Sin is falling short of anything which is right in God's sight (Rom. 3:23). The Bible says that "all have sinned." Does that mean me? Does it mean you? Make each person see from the Bible account that all *have* sinned. After asking them if lying is a sin, you might ask that those who have never sinned raise their hand. Sometimes a hand or two will go up, usually from the younger children. Then ask each one pointedly, "Have you ever gotten a spanking?" All will say "yes." Then ask *why* they got a spanking; with their reply say, "And that is sin, isn't it?" Watch their faces until you see the convicting power of the Spirit working in each heart. Repeat a number of times that no one who has not received the Lord Jesus, or trusted in Jesus, can go to heaven. But God knew that we would sin, and in His love, He provided an answer for the sin in our hearts. (Turn over to the red page.)

The Red Page — The BLOOD OF JESUS (Present here the gospel: I Cor. 15:3-4)

Now you are ready to present Christ to the children. It is good to stay on the black page until the child sees that "being good" will not save him. There are no good works that can take away sin.

Tell them that the red page stands for Jesus' blood (I John 1:7). God loved us so very much that He sent Jesus from heaven to earth to die on the cross for us. Explain that Jesus on the cross took all our sins. God put all of our sins upon Jesus there. All His suffering was for us. Sin is so bad that only Jesus could take our sins away.

Make it clear that Jesus on the cross did all that was needed to take away our sins. He saves, and He alone (Acts 4:12; Eph. 2:8-9). Show how Christ substituted for us on the cross. (Turn to the white page.)

The White Page — CLEAN HEARTS (through accepting Jesus as Saviour)

Stress the resurrection in the Gospel (I Cor. 15:3-4). The teacher should make clear to the children that while Jesus died for our sins, we *must* accept Him, believe on Him, or call upon Him to save us (John 1:12; Acts 16:31; Rom. 10:13). When we do, He takes away our sins instantly. The white page stands for our hearts washed clean when God saves us (Ps. 51:7). He makes us as white as snow (Isa. 1:18).

At this point each child should be asked to invite Christ into his heart as Saviour and Lord. The teacher should make this very personal. Have the children close their eyes, so that there is no "following the leader mass movement." He may ask all who desire Jesus to come into their hearts now (using Rev. 3:20 as the closing appeal) to raise their hands for prayer, then put them down. In certain situations it might be better to ask all who would like Jesus to come into their hearts now and save them, to get up and follow the teacher out of the room. In any case, after the teacher has the children to be dealt with aside, the gospel is again presented, questions are asked, then each child should be asked to pray personally, first thanking Jesus for dying for their sins on the cross and, secondly, asking Jesus to come into their hearts, right now, and take their sins away. The teacher can be alert in this personal atmosphere to any child who does not seem serious or has yet to realize what Christ has done. Questions should now be asked, helping the child toward assurance. Again, the teacher never tells a child he is "saved." This is the Spirit's work.

Ask the children, "Suppose you sin again?" Then teach them instant confession (I John 1:9), daily prayer, and the need for Bible reading for Christian growth (turn to the green page).

The Green Page — The Christian LIFE (a life of growth)

Many living, growing things in the great outdoors are green, such as the hedges and grass, and trees. The Christian life is also a life of growth. When we receive Jesus into our hearts as Saviour, life has just begun, a life of growth. God wants us to grow in grace (II Pet. 3:18). We get our Christian food for growth through the Bible (I Pet. 2:2).

As time permits, take up a study of those things which help us to grow; yielding ourselves wholly to God each day (Rom. 12:1-2), confessing Christ to others in daily witnessing (Matt. 10:32), studying God's Word (Acts 17:11); praying to the Lord (Matt. 7:7), meeting weekly with God's people at church (Heb. 10:25), living to please Jesus and obeying our parents (Col. 3:17; Eph. 6:1).

Fasten the meaning of each page in the minds of the children. Secure copies of the Wordless Book (Printers: Child Evangelism Fellowship, Grand Rapids, Mich.), or help those saved to make them and carry them with them everywhere for witnessing. Contests and special study groups for children on how to use the Wordless Book for witnessing to parents and friends have been found most helpful.

It should be the goal of the pastor that everyone in his church be able to give either the Wordless Book or the "Bridge of Life" Illustration, according to their age and ability. To equip each member with some tool for personal witnessing is the *first* step toward a total witnessing church.

HOW TO HAVE A DAILY "QUIET TIME"

God wants to give us "marching orders" for the day (Ps. 37:23). He seeks fellowship with us — knowing the coldness of our hearts toward Him (I Cor. 1:9).

Helps for a successful daily "quiet time" with God (see also pp. 196-197):

1. Pick a definite time; decide the night before *when* you are going to meet the Lord. Choose the best time for you individually. Most people are too tired at night successfully to meet and gain vital contact with the Lord. The purpose for any time with God should first be to "know Him" and to experience through faith His divine presence.

2. Pick a definite place. A place secluded from the noise of the children or interruptions is best; perhaps it will be a small room, basement, car, or closet. Get *alone* with God. Family devotions are important, but they do not take the place of a personal time with God.

3. Have definite things in mind:

a. Use the prayer list idea. Make up a list of the things that God puts on your heart; this way, whether you "feel" like praying or not, you can ask the Lord in faith and He will answer your prayers. Be flexible. Change your list regularly; you don't have to use it, but it is there when your heart is cold and you don't *feel* prayerful. Remember, God doesn't answer because we "feel" we are being heard, but because we are believing Him (Matt. 21:22).

b. Use the Word of God. George Muller, the famous prayer warrior for God, used to say that reading and studying the Word *before* you pray prepares you for believing God and really getting answers from Him. Sometimes it is best to read a chapter slowly, praying over each verse. Ask God to make it real and personal to your heart. Have a definite passage selected before you start your "quiet time." "The most time wasted is the time wasted getting started." Work out a schedule of reading a chapter or a book of the Bible to go along with your time with God. If you are a new Christian, concentrate on the letters of Paul. These were some of the first books of the New Testament to be written, especially for new converts.

GUIDANCE

The principle of divine guidance in our daily life is important not only to us personally but it is also a dynamic factor in our relationships with other people, particularly those we seek to disciple. The trainer of men must build into his own life the habitual "waiting on God" to receive directed guidance about everything he does during the day.

If we do not have His peace, then we must stop and ask for His guidance.

Running ahead of God is as dangerous as being out of step with Him. David prayed, "Cause me to hear thy loving-kindness in the morning, for in thee do I trust: cause me to know the way wherein I should walk; for I lift up my soul unto thee" (Ps. 143:8). Examples and illustrations of specific guidance in the Scriptures are many. The Holy Spirit desires to lead us moment by moment into God's perfect way of life (Rom. 8:14).

Some helpful suggestions for getting His guidance are:

1. *Stop.* When you are not clear on His revealed will, it is useless to advance. Let your heart seek the face of God in quietness.

2. *Look.* Open the Word of God and look for His message to your heart. Read and meditate specifically in books dealing with the devotional life and the will of God: Psalms, Proverbs, Philippians, etc., are good. Note the promises in James 1:5; Philippians 2:13; Isaiah 32:17; Psalm 37:3-5.

3. *Listen.* Take time to listen for God's speaking to your heart. Take time enough to forget time. Seek out what God has to say to you.

4. *Write it down.* Capture each thought on paper; this leaves you free for the next one. Some are not worth capturing, but some are. We can't be sure until we take the next step.

5. *Test it.* The test for guidance is always the Word of God. He will never lead us contrary to His Word. A basic question is: Is the thought that comes up in me full of faith, love, honesty, purity, unselfishness? God never leads away from these absolutes that were so much a part of the life of our Lord. Guidance is always toward Christlikeness in ourselves and towards others.

6. *Take the step.* After the guidance has passed the Scripture test, seek God's face for what the next step will be.

Where do I go from here? How do I start? What is the deepest need for now? God's order is always perfect and complete in every way.

7. *Obey*. Absolute obedience to His revealed will is the foundation for all other guidance. God cannot trust us with decisions which affect not only men but nations, until we are willing to yield to Him daily in the "little things." The Holy Spirit does not work automatically; there must be a conscious yielding to and dependence upon Him for His work. Trust Him to guide wisely. Guidance will always be from God's viewpoint, and therefore at times it will conflict completely with the "normal pattern" of the world.

APPENDIX C

SUPPLEMENTARY LESSONS FOR THE
NEW MEMBER CLASS

These seven lessons are intended as a supplement for a New Member class the pastor may already be teaching, and will extend the class to ten to twelve weeks. They may be used as Unit I, stressing the Christian's relationship and responsibility to Christ. The pastor can then select his own material in Unit II on the Christian's relationship and responsibility to his church.

Unit II lessons were not included because of varying individual and denominational doctrinal emphases.

Whereas all new members might be reluctant to attend a class where only familiar church ordinances and organizations are taught, Unit I is designed to attract both new believers and new members. The lessons are accompanied by outside assignments and are designed to meet some of the immediate needs of both groups.

With this foundation the Christian will be much more responsive to the church's mission, ordinances, organizations and stewardship.

CLASS I

NEW LIFE FOR YOU

Goal: To present the Gospel clearly so that students know the fundamentals of salvation.

Key verse: John 5:24: Assurance of Salvation.

Illustrative material: "Bridge of Life" illustration, pp. 172-177.

Contents:

Introduction to Growth: When a person is born into this world, he is a baby; when he is born again by the Holy Spirit, he is likewise a baby in the spiritual realm. No matter what his maturity or knowledge in other areas, spiritually he must start at the beginning. Also, many believers who have been Christians for a long time are still babies because they have remained immature. Physical growth is never automatic; it is dependent upon food, air, rest, and exercise. Growing in spiritual maturity, i.e. Christlikeness, comes only through daily application of what is learned from the Bible and through prayer (Heb. 5:12-14).

Some characteristics of spiritual babies are: (1) they are helpless and dependent upon others for their needs; (2) they expect attention, desiring always to be the center of interest in their little world; (3) they live in the surface realm of feeling and become moody if they don't get everything they desire; (4) they lack discernment between good and bad; (5) they are not able to reproduce themselves. Before we as "babes in Christ" can grow we must understand the simple story of salvation and make sure that we see clearly our new relationship to our heavenly Father, the church, His people, and the world.

I. *"Bridge of Life" Illustration.* Present this illustration slowly and carefully. Have the class turn to the Scriptures with you, and have them draw out the illustration as you draw it before them. Make sure they understand the gospel (I Cor. 15:1-4).

II. *Memory Work.* Stress Scripture memorization; explain the great value of hiding God's Word in the heart. Assign John 5:24, the key verse in the "Bridge" for their first memory project. Emphasize the importance of also memorizing the topic with the verse. The teacher would do well to have cards available in class so that each student may print the verse before leaving.

A. The memorized Word is an aid to walking in victory over self and Satan. Illustrate with Matthew 4:1-11; Psalm 119:9,11.

B. The memorized Word helps us to learn the Bible more quickly. Illustrate the value of knowing a key verse in a passage which will help us to remember the context of the whole section. Memory is therefore a great help to Bible teaching (Col. 3:16).

C. For further suggestions on the "how" of Scripture memory see page 163.

III. *Assignments.*

A. Memorize John 5:24 with its topic, "Assurance of Salvation."

B. Write out the "Bridge Illustration" at least four times during the week. Write it from memory first, as best as you can, then check it with your class copy, and so on. You need not memorize the references at this time; however, they should be looked up and marked in your Bible along with the page numbers of the next verses. Be prepared to draw out the basic illustration next class period.

C. Do at least three questions a day in the first Gospel of John study (pp. 141ff.). "Eating the Word of God" daily is fundamental to Christian growth and service. Set a definite time for daily memorization, study, and private prayer.

IV. *Testimony and Sentence Prayer.* Give opportunity for a new Christian to share his experience of conversion. Encourage everyone to pray at least one sentence publicly. Call each class member during the week to encourage them in their Bible study. Ask if there is any question you might help them with or problem which you might help them solve.

CLASS II

ASSURANCE

Goal: To present the keeping work of Christ in salvation, so that each class member has assurance of his relationship to Christ.

Key verse: I John 5:11,12: Assurance of Salvation.

Illustrative material: Bridge Assurance Illustration (p. 177).

Contents:

I. *Review.* About one-third of each class time should be spent in reviewing.

    A. Determine how many learned John 5:24, completed the John Bible study, and can draw out the Bridge Illustration.

    B. Have the class quote together John 5:24.

    C. Ask for a volunteer to draw the Bridge Illustration; have the class help fill in the illustration as needed. Question the class on their grasp of the gospel.

    D. The teacher may desire to make attendance slips with a place to record assignments completed; thus a record may be kept privately on the progress of each student.

II. *A New Creation and a New Life.*

    A. The new birth we experienced in salvation (John 3:1-16) brings us a completely new life (II Cor. 5:17; Gal. 6:15).

        1. We have new affections (Matt. 22:37; II Cor. 5:14,15).

        2. We have a new Lord (I Cor. 15:47; Acts 10:36; Rom. 10:11-13).

        3. We have a new standard — Christ and the Bible. Christ is our all in all. We look to Him (I. Pet. 2:21; Heb. 1:12; 13:8). The Bible is our authority (II Tim. 3:16; Heb. 4:12; II Pet. 1:20, 21; Isaiah 8:20).

        4. We have a new family — the family of God, made up of all believers in Christ, with God as our Fath-

er. We are the "body of Christ"; He is our "head." We are His children by faith alone (Rom. 8:16,17; Gal. 3:26; John 1:11-13).

   5. We have a new life — Jesus Christ is our Life (II Cor. 13:5; Col. 1:27; 3:4; John 15:5).

  B. The new birth we experienced in salvation brings us to a completely new relationship with the Holy Spirit.

   1. He is a Person (John 16:13; 14:26).

   2. He indwells every believer (I Cor. 3:16; 6:19; John 14:17; Rom. 8:9). He seeks to "control" (translated "filled" in Ephesians 5:18) our lives moment by moment so we will continually glorify Christ (John 15:26; 16:14; Phil. 1:20, 21).

III. *Illustration.* Present the Bridge Assurance Illustration. Point out how the Holy Spirit is the Agent of salvation, bringing us *to* Christ, putting us *in* Christ, and keeping us *for* Christ.

IV. *Assurance.* After the presentation, seek by questions to determine whether all in the class do have assurance. Remember, assurance is the work of the Holy Spirit, who uses the Word (I. Thess. 1:5,6); the key verse, I John 5:11,12, indicates that Christ *is* life. Eternal life is in a Person; to have Christ is to have His life! Other helpful verses on assurance are John 1:11-13; I John 5:13.

  A. Since the first attack of Satan usually is against the believer's assurance, indicate for the class the divine order: fact, faith, then feeling. We must not measure our salvation by our feelings or the lack of them.

  B. The Bible alone is our standard for assurance. Paul feared that his converts should trust in men instead of in God for their assurance (I Cor. 2:1-5). What God says remains true and sure (Matt. 24:35; Isaiah 40:6-8).

V. *Assignments.*

  A. Learn to give the Assurance Illustration.

B. Memorize I John 5:11,12; review your other verse, John 5:24.

C. Turn in John study No. 1; fill in John study No. 2 at the rate of at least 3 questions each day.

VI. *Prayer and Testimony.* Encourage prayer and testimonies to God's faithfulness and answers to prayer during the past week. The teacher may start this closing part of the class by sharing some precious recent blessing from God in his life.

VII. *Preview.* To keep up the interest of the class, preview some of the coming topics.

CLASS III

CHRIST OUR LIFE

Goal: To illustrate to the believer his relationship to Christ as the Center of his life. This relationship enables him to live the Spirit-filled, victorious, fruitful Christian life.

Key verse: Matthew 6:33: Putting Christ First.

Illustrative Material: Bridge Assurance Illustration (p. 177).

Review: 1. Quote I John 5:11,12 aloud.

2. Go over some of the content of John study No. 2; stress the unique Deity of Christ; ask questions of the class.

Contents:

I. *The Christ-Centered Life.*

Have the class draw out with you the "wheel" illustration. This illustration is best presented by showing the definite dependence of each spoke on the other three spokes, and the interdependence of all the parts of Christ as Center and Lord.

II. *Assignments:*

1. Memorize Matthew 6:33 and I Corinthians 10:13: Assurance of Victory.

2. Review and learn to draw out the Christ-Centered Life

Illustration. Meditate on the relation of each spoke to Christ.

3. Fill in John study No. 3; during the week call one class member and share some blessing from your study.

CLASS IV

FORGIVENESS

Goal: To teach the doctrines of forgiveness from sin, of confession and restoration to fellowship with Christ.

Key verse: I John 1:9

Contents:

I. *Forgiveness.*

For the believer, I John 1:9 is one of the most important verses in the Bible. The truth taught there is essential for the believer's daily relationship with Christ. For the surrendered Christian, sin is no longer a necessity; but when he does fall into sin, the Bible makes adequate provision for sins committed.

A. The *basis* for forgiveness is the "blood of Christ" (John 1:7). Jesus is the "Lamb of God" who died for our sins (John 1:29).

1. Forgiveness through the offering of a lamb is pictured in the Old Testament (Exod. 12:1-14; Lev. 16:2-3,24; Hos. 28:2-4; Isa. 53).

2. Forgiveness by God is instant (John 20:31; Isa. 1:18; I Pet. 2:24; Matt. 27:51). There is no waiting for God to forgive; we "confess our sins" and He is "faithful and just to forgive."

3. Forgiveness is complete and full. There is no halfway forgiveness with God because Christ was sacrificed for *all* sin once, completing the payment for sin before God (Heb. 9:26-28; 10:10,14,17-20).

4. Forgiveness means our sins are forgotten, hidden under the shed blood of Christ (Jer. 31:34; Isa. 38:17; 44:22; Col. 2:14).

B. To be forgiven we must *confess* our sins. To confess means "to say with God," to call sin what God calls it. Saying "I have sinned" is not confession so much as calling out to God that specific sin of which we are being convicted by Him. We are "agreeing with God" that our transgression is sin. No one can truly confess his sins without being conscious of them. General confession, as in some public prayers, means little unless the person prays knowingly, "saying with God" what his sins are. Sin is a pointed, specific thing; so must be the confession.

C. To be restored to fellowship with God (which sin instantly breaks), we need to confess our sins as we are convicted of them. Even waiting until evening for prayer and confession is not according to the will of God. God hates sin; it separates us from His fellowship. Instant confession means instant restoration with God. The most important thing in all the world is unbroken communion with our heavenly Father.

One woman asked her pastor, "Does we confess 'em as we does 'em, or does we bunch 'em?" That was a very good question. Let us not be guilty of "bunching" our sins for confession. Restoration can be ours immediately when we confess. Confessing sin implies a rejection of that sin from our lives, and a turning in trust to the Spirit whose power we must experience for victory over sin.

D. There is a very practical aspect of God's forgiveness of our sins. We must forgive others as God forgives, instantly, and forget the transgression toward us as far as it affects our attitudes toward a person.

1. Unconfessed sin blocks the way to receive a blessing in Bible study and prayer (Ps. 66:18; Prov. 28:9,13).

2. Our unwillingness to forgive others implies that we consider someone's sin against us greater than our sin against God! Note in Colossians 3:12-16 and

194 *New Testament Follow-Up*

Ephesians 4:30-32 the sins which grieve the Spirit.
3. We are told to "cleanse ourselves" (Jas. 4:8). This does not mean that we can work for forgiveness, or that we have any power in ourselves to achieve it. We must "judge ourselves" (I Cor. 11:31) before we are judged by God. We are "cleansed" through the Word of God implanted experimentally and consistently in our hearts (John 15:3; Eph. 5:26-27; Ps. 119:11).

III. *Assignments.*
1. Memorize I John 1:9.
2. Complete John study 4.
3. Be able to answer questions about forgiveness from your class notes and through meditation on I John 1:9.
4. Review the "wheel" illustration, noting how sin destroys the effectiveness of all four spokes relating to Christ.

CLASS V

GRASPING THE WORD OF GOD

Goal: To illustrate and explain the various parts of the "Word spoke" from the Wheel illustration to help the students to evaluate their personal life in relation to their feeding on God's Word.

Key verse: Psa. 119:9,11: Walking in Victory.

Illustrative material: The "hand" illustration (pp. 130-135).

Review: Have the class members draw the Christ-Centered Life Illustration. Have a discussion on just how sin blocks the effectiveness of the Word, prayer, obedience, and witnessing in the life. Then write out I John 1:9 for memory and answer the following questions: (a) What does "confess" mean? (b) When should we confess and why? (c) What happens to the sins we do not know we commit, if we confess our known sins?

Contents:

I. *The Hand Illustration.* Teach this illustration from the material in the Appendix, showing the five avenues God has given us for getting a grasp on His Word. Use Scriptures.
   A. Have the class draw out the illustration in their notebooks.
   B. Go over at least one verse per finger in detail.
   C. Stress how useless all fingers are without the thumb; relate meditation to each finger.

II. *The "hearing" finger.*
   A. Emphasize that "listening is not necessarily learning." Discuss briefly Mark 8:17,18 on hearing the Word.
      1. Discuss the practical application of hearing the Word through note taking at church worship services, etc. The average member hears at least 50 to 150 messages per year. Few will recall any detail of even five messages. Pass out sample note taking sheets from Appendix A.
      2. To help the class members take effective notes the following suggestions are given:
         a. Teach the class how to outline (individually as needed).
         b. Decide what you want them to jot down:
            (1) Scripture references, (2) titles and subtitles, (3) basic sentences, (4) vivid illustrations, (5) definitions of words in a verse.
         c. Have them write down ideas rather than word-for-word sentences.
         d. Teach them to listen for truths applicable to their own needs as God speaks through His Word.
         e. They can use a notebook or file box for their notes; file under topics or books of the Bible.
         f. Underline that they should review meaningful notes and apply them to their personal life until

they are a part of their own thinking and life; throw away notes no longer useful, or those already applied, after a few months. The best way to "keep" your notes is to share them immediately with another.

g. Teach the class how to abbreviate the books of the Bible and tell them to write smaller when taking notes; this will increase speed in writing.

h. Practice note taking with them by listening to a tape or speaker, then share your notes with them.

III. *The "reading" finger.* Present to the class the helpful suggestions on how to get more from purposeful Bible reading (p. 135). Encourage them to use these suggestions with their regular Bible reading this next week.

IV. *Assignments.*

1. Take notes on at least one message before next class and come prepared to share them.

2. Complete John study No. 5; turn in study No. 4 to the teacher.

3. Memorize Psalm 119:9,11: Walking in Victory. Review every day all other verses that have been assigned.

CLASS VI

VICTORIOUS PRAYER

Goal: To help class members start and maintain a consistent "quiet time" or period of daily devotions.

Key verse: John 16:24. Assurance of Provision.

Review: After going over the assignments from last time, re-emphasize the Christ-Centered Life Illustration in relation to the "prayer spoke."

Contents:

I. *The "Quiet Time."* Use the material on pages 182ff. as source material.

A. The class should be warned that Satan's attack here is to occupy them continually with things to *do* rather than pray. Aside from feeding on the Word, no habit of the spiritual life is more important to maintain, or more difficult to establish than a daily "quiet time."

B. Why do I need a "quiet time"?
   1. For fellowship with the Lord Jesus (I Cor. 1:9).
   2. For peace of mind and soul (Phil. 4:6.7; I Pet. 5:7).
   3. For direction, guidance, and clarity of purpose and goal for each day (Ps. 143:8; 37:23).
   4. For praise and worship (John 4:23; Ps. 107:15; 34:1).
   5. For meditation and the consciousness of His presence (I Chron. 16:10-12; Prov. 22:17-19; Ps. 1:2; Josh. 1:8).
C. How to set up a daily "quiet time." Use Appendix notes.

III. *Assignments.*
   1. Make out a prayer list for each day of the week; set up a minimum devotional period of at least fifteen minutes.
   2. Memorize John 16:24 and Matthew 21:22; write down the names of three unsaved contacts or friends, and remember them daily this coming week according to these verses.
   3. Complete John study No. 6.
   4. Emphasize consistent Bible reading; go over a daily Bible reading guide with them, using denominational literature or your own plan.

CLASS VII
WITNESSING FOR CHRIST

Goal: To teach each believer his responsibility, opportunity, and the necessity to witness; make practical suggestions on having a Biblical witness.

Key verse: Psalm 107:2. Telling About Him.

Review: Find out about their success with their "quiet time." Go over any problems brought out; share any personal blessing which God brought to your heart during your "quiet time." Quote John 16:24 and Matthew 21:22 aloud together. Check whether they have yet begun to pray for at least three unsaved people by name. Provide names from the church prospect list or known unsaved church contacts so that everyone has at least three people on his daily prayer list.

I. *The responsibility of every believer to witness.*
   A. In John 15:16 we are told to "go and bring forth fruit." One of the fruits of the spiritual life is witnessing. This fruit is different from the "fruit of the Spirit" (Gal. 5:22, 23), which can be experienced without "going" anywhere. But God seeks obedient believers who as His disciples go forth to witness for Him.
   B. The man in right relatonship with God is a tree of life (Prov. 11:30). Sowing the seed of the Word of God (Ps. 126:5,6; Mark 4:14) can bring forth a whole tree full of fruit, not just one fruit or soul. Proper sowing means multiplication of souls to the glory of God. Only through the multiplication of saved souls can we reach a multiplying world.
   C. We have been commissioned (Matt. 28:19,20) to do what Jesus taught His disciples to do (John 20:21); our mission is the same mission God sent Jesus to do (Luke 19:10; I Tim. 1:15). Witnessing is our responsibility.
   D. Winning the lost to Christ is the normal overflow of the daily life in Christ. Fruit is excess life. When we are in His will, God brings forth fruit through us.

II. *Present the Bridge of Life Illustration again to the class.* Review this useful tool to evangelism. By this time they should be able to present it well. Emphasize the relation of Scripture to the written illustration. Everyone should know a few Scriptures if they are ever to win a soul. This illustration enables them to tie some of these Scriptures together and present the gospel with greater clarity. Stress that no one grouping of Scriptures, or any illustration in itself, is sufficient for every situation. Salvation is in the Son, not in a plan in itself. When most of the class members can draw the Bridge and have used it with an unsaved person, present the Wordless Book illustration from Appendix B.

III. *Teach the class how to give a scriptural testimony.* Explain the difference between witnessing, a testimony, and presenting the gospel.

   A. Witnessing is the total impact of the individual believer's life and speech, both positively and negatively (Phil. 2:15,16).

   B. A testimony is telling someone what Jesus has done in and for you. It involves these four divisions found in Acts 26:1-23 and Acts 22:1-30:

      1. Something of my life before Jesus became my Saviour and Lord of my life (Acts 22:1-5).

      2. How and when I trusted Christ (Acts 22:6-10).

      3. Something of the change He has made in me, my home life, work, school, friends, attitudes, etc. (Acts 22:14-21; 26:19-24).

      4. A definite invitation that those to whom I am speaking accept Jesus as their Lord (Acts 26:25-30).

   C. The gospel is Christ's life, His death for our sins on the cross, His burial, and His resurrection (I Cor. 15:1-4). Every Christian should know the minimum scriptural gospel in this passage for personal witnessing. Many witnesses are not effective because they take for granted that their listener knows the facts of the gospel. When the gospel is presented it is powerful (Rom. 1:16). It may be combined with a testimony, or the testimony may be given first as the witness seeks to determine the guidance of the Spirit in presenting the gospel to the listener.

   D. Jesus must always be the center of any witness or gospel message if the power of the Spirit is to bring conviction to the listener. The Spirit convicts the unsaved of the sin of "unbelief" (John 16:8-11). Effective witnessing is always Christ-centered (I Cor. 2:2).

IV. *Where and when to witness.* The class should be taught the four "worlds" of our witness: the home, the neighborhood, the place of employment, and the social world. Show the class some opportunities open to them for witnessing in each of these areas.

V. *Assignments.*

1. Present the Bridge illustration to some unsaved friend or neighbor; perhaps it might be the one for whom you have been praying this past week.

2. Some class members may prefer to present the Wordless Book to some contact or child. Both of these valuable tools should be part of each member's spiritual witness.

3. Memorize at least three of the verses in the Bridge illustration; plan to know them all within two weeks.

4. Write out your testimony on paper. Be prepared to share it with the rest of the class. The teacher may desire to give a brief three-minute testimony before the end of the class by way of illustration to the students. The testimony need not follow the pattern given previously but should be written prayerfully and in plain language. Three words might characterize a good testimony: It should present the "before," "how," and "now."

Note: The teacher may now desire to go into Unit II with its special denominational-doctrinal instruction emphasis. It would be useful if he could continue to give some small weekly assignment and to check that it is done. Before the class returns to the regular groups where they will hereafter minister, the need for workers in the Adoption Plan visitation of other new members should be emphasized. Those who have been diligent in their assignments will make good follow-up visitors to future new members. Perhaps the last ten minutes of the final class period should be given to introducing a representative from each age group of the Sunday school or evening training hour. Let them tell where their group meets, how to get there, and give a personal word of welcome to the new members in their age group.

BIBLIOGRAPHY

Anderson, R. A., *The Shepherd-Evangelist*, Washington: Review & Herald Publishers, 1950.

Autrey, C. E., *Basic Evangelism*, Grand Rapids: Zondervan Publishing House, 1959.

Archibald, A. C., *Establishing the Convert*, Philadelphia: Judson Press, 1952.

Bounds, E. M., *The Preacher and Prayer*, Grand Rapids: Zondervan Publishing House, 1946.

Chambers, Oswald, *So Send I You*, London: Marshall, Morgan & Scott, 1951.

Conant, J. E., *Every-Member Evangelism*, New York: Harper & Brothers, 1922.

Cook, Bob, *Now That I Believe*, Chicago: Moody Press.

Davidson, Francis, *The New Bible Commentary*, Grand Rapids: Wm. B. Eerdmans Publishing Co., 1956.

Eavey, C. B., *The Art of Effective Teaching*, Grand Rapids: Zondervan Publishing House, 1953.

Farrar, F. W., *The Life and Work of Paul*, London: Cassell and Company.

Fickett, Harold L., *Baptist Beliefs*, Nashville: Broadman Press.

Gregory, John M., *The Seven Laws of Teaching*, Grand Rapids: Baker Book House, 1956.

Grindstaff, W. E., *Ways to Win*, Nashville: Broadman Press, 1957.

Hay, Alexander R., *The New Testament Order for Church and Missionary*, The Netherlands: H. H. Blok, 1947.

Hogg and Vine, *The Epistles to the Thessalonians*, Fincastle, Va.: Bible Study Classics Reprint, 1959.

Huegel, F. J., *Bone of His Bone*, Grand Rapids: Zondervan Publishing House.

Kernaban, A. E., *Visitation Evangelism,* New York: Fleming H. Ravell, 1925.

Leavell, Roland Q., *The Romance of Evangelism,* New York: Fleming H. Revell, 1942.

Mangum, O. R., *Paul's Swan Song,* Grand Rapids: Zondervan Publishing House, 1941.

Martin, T. T., *God's Plan with Men,* New York: Loizeaux Brothers Inc.

Morling, G. H., *The Quest for Serenity,* Grand Rapids: Wm. Eerdmans Publishing Co.

Moody, D. L., *Pleasure and Profit in Bible Study,* New York: Fleming H. Revell, 1895.

Moore, W. B., "Evangelism In Depth," *The Baptist Standard,* Dallas, March, 1960.

Murray, Andrew, *Abide in Christ,* New York: Grossit & Dunlap.

Murray, Andrew, *The Ministry of Intercession,* New York: Fleming H. Revell.

Murray, Andrew, *The School of Obedience,* New York: Fleming H. Revell, 1899.

Patterson, Alexander, *Bird's-Eye Bible Study,* Chicago: Moody Press, 1911.

Paxon, Ruth, *Life on the Highest Plane,* Chicago: Moody Press, 1928.

Powell, S. W., *Where Are the Converts,* Nashville: Broadman Press, 1958.

Ramm, Bernard, *Protestant Bibical Interpretation,* Boston: W. A. Wilde Publishers, 1956.

Sanderson, Leonard, *Personal Evangelism,* Nashville: Convention Press, 1958.

Shoemaker, Samuel M., *Revive Thy Church Beginning with Me,* New York: Harper & Brothers, 1948.

Sullivan, James, *Your Life and Your Church,* Nashville, Convention Press.

Smith, Hannah W., *The Christian's Secret of a Happy Life,* Westwood, N.J., Fleming H. Revell, 1952.

Stott, John R., *Basic Christianity,* Grand Rapids: Wm. B. Eerdmans Publishing Co., 1958.

Thomas, W. H. Griffith, *Methods of Bible Study,* Chicago: Moody Press, 1926.

Thomas, W. H. Griffith, *The Christian Life and How To Live It,* Chicago: Moody Press, 1919.

Trotman, Dawson, *Born to Reproduce,* Lincoln, Nebraska: Back to the Bible Publishers, 1957.

Trumbull, C. G., *The Life That Wins,* Philadelphia: The Sunday School Times, 1958.

The Treasury of Scripture Knowledge, Westwood, N.J.: Fleming H. Revell.

The New Testament, Charles Williams; Chicago: Moody Press, 1958.

Weiss, G. C., *On Being a Real Christian,* Chicago: Moody Press, 1952.

Young's Analytical Concordance to the Bible, Grand Rapids: Wm. B. Eerdmans Publishing Co.